Judges:

Disobedience, Departure, Discipline & Deliverance

Ken Fleming

Developed as a study course by Emmaus Correspondence School, founded in 1942.

Mission

Glorify God by providing biblically sound resources and structured study materials that teach people from every nation to accept Christ as their Savior and Lord, grow in Christ and share their faith with others.

Judges: Disobedience, Departure, Discipline, & Deliverance

Ken Fleming

Published by:
Emmaus Worldwide
PO Box 1028
Dubuque, IA 52004-1028
phone: (563) 585-2070
email: info@emmausworldwide.org
website: EmmausWorldwide.org

First Edition 2012 (AK '12), 2 Units
Reprinted 2017 (AK '12), 2 Units
Reprinted 2018 (AK '18), 2 Units
Revised 2020 (AK '20), 2 Units
Reprinted 2022 (AK '20), 2 Units

ISBN 978-1-59387-089-8

Code: JUDG

Printed in the United States of America

Course Overview

The book of Judges records the history of the nation of Israel in the Promised Land from the death of Joshua until just prior to the kingdom being established under King Saul. During this period, the nation failed God repeatedly, prompting Him to allow the pagan people in the land and surrounding areas to oppress them. Whenever Israel cried out to God for help, He would graciously raise up leaders to deliver them from their enemies and a time of peace would come—until the next time they failed.

The writer of Judges appears to have had a threefold purpose in recording this sad history:

- To demonstrate the effects of a godless culture on His people.
- To explain the necessity for God's judgment on those who compromised His holy standards.
- To show that God was faithful to His covenant with His chosen people, even though they sinned.

Lessons You Will Study

Student Instructions

This Emmaus course is designed to help you know God through a better understanding of the Bible and know it applies to your life. However, this course can never take the place of the Bible itself. The Bible is inexhaustible, and no course can give the full meaning of its truth. If simply studying this course is the end goal, it will become an obstacle to your growth; if it is used to inspire and equip you for your own personal study of the Bible, then it will achieve its goal. As you study the Bible using this course, prayerfully ask God to reveal His truth to you in a powerful way.

Course Sections

This course has three parts: the *lessons*, the *exams* and the *answer sheet*.

The Lessons

Each lesson is written to help explain truths from the Bible. Read each lesson through at least twice—once to get a general idea of its content, then again, slowly, looking up any Bible references given. You should always have your Bible opened to the verses or passage being studied. It is important that you read the Bible passages referenced, as some questions in the exams may be based on the Bible text.

To look up a Bible verse, keep in mind that passages in the Bible are listed by book, chapter, and verse. For instance, 2 Peter 1:21 refers to the second book of Peter, chapter 1, and verse 21. At the beginning of every Bible, there is a table of contents which lists the names of the books of the Bible and tells the page number on which each book begins. For practice, look up 2 Peter in the table of contents, turn to the page number listed, then find the chapter and verse.

The Exams

At the end of each lesson, there is an exam to assess your knowledge of the course material and the Bible passages. The exams contain multiple choice and/or True/False (T/F) questions. After you have studied a lesson, complete the exam for that lesson by recording your answers on the exam sheet that has been provided. If you have difficulty answering the questions, re-read the lesson or use the Bible as a reference.

Please note, it is best not to answer the questions based on what you *think* or have *always believed*. The questions are designed to find out if you understand the material in the course and the Bible.

What Do You Say?

In addition to the multiple choice section, each exam also contains a *What Do You Say?* question. These questions are designed for your personal reflection and to help you express your ideas and feelings as you process the lesson's content.

The Answer Sheet

Use the answer sheet provided by your group leader or instructor. When you have determined the right answer to a question on an exam, fill in the corresponding letter on the answer sheet. If you do not have someone who could provide an answer sheet, you can download one at www.emmausworldwide.org/answersheets

Submitting the Answer Sheet

When you have answered all the exam questions on the answer sheet, check them carefully. Fill in your contact information and submit your completed answer sheet to your group leader or instructor or the organization from which you received it (several options for submission are shown on next page).

OPTION 1: Send to your group leader or instructor

If you know your group leader or instructor, give them your completed answer sheet or mail it to the address listed here (if blank, go to option 2).

OPTION 2: Send to Emmaus Worldwide's head office

If no address is listed above, or if you do not know if you have a group leader or instructor and are unsure of where to send your answer sheet, choose one of the following:

MAIL the exam sheet to

Emmaus Worldwide
PO Box 1028
Dubuque, IA 52004-1028

EMAIL the exam sheet to

Exams@EmmausWorldwide.org

Receiving Your Results

You will receive back your graded exam sheet (through the same method it was submitted, either mail or email), including your final grade and a personal response from your group leader or instructor or a representative of Emmaus Worldwide.

LESSON 1

The Broken Covenant

Judges 1:1–2:5

Introduction

The book of Judges records the history of the nation of Israel in their land from the death of Joshua to just prior to the establishment of the kingdom under King Saul. Joshua had defeated the nations in Canaan and subdued the whole land by the power of God (though there were still pockets of resistance in certain areas). Each tribe was then allotted an area in which to settle. There was no national leader to replace Joshua, but God graciously raised up twelve leaders at special times to deliver the tribes from the oppression of their enemies that they brought on themselves because of their repeated rebellion against God. These twelve were called *judges,* though their activities were military and political rather than judicial (2:16-18; Ruth 1:1). Their lives contained many obvious flaws, making it all the more remarkable that four of them are mentioned among the heroes of faith in Hebrews 11:32.

The events recorded in the book are arranged in a series of repeated cycles.

From Disobedience to Deliverance

The events recorded in the book are arranged in a series of repeated cycles that begin with the Israelites' *disobedience* to God's command to completely drive out the Canaanites. In their disobedience they also turned away, *departing* from God to adopt the idolatry of the pagan Canaanites.

God responded to their disobedience with *discipline* by allowing their enemies to attack them, defeat them, and oppress them until their lives were miserable. Then, when they cried out to God to save them, He sent a judge (or savior) to *deliver* them from their enemies. Their deliverance was followed by a period of peace and rest. This pattern of events became a cycle repeated seven times in the book:

1. The people's disobedience
2. The people's departure
3. God's discipline
4. God's deliverance

The Israelite tribes were fairly faithful to God during the lifetime of Joshua and of his appointed elders, a period that ended about 1350 BC (Josh. 24:31; Judges 2:7). The period of the judges continued for over three hundred years until Saul was made king, about 1050 BC. However, an accurate chronology of the period is not possible from the biblical record. The book of Judges was probably written in the early years of David's reign, perhaps by the prophet Samuel.

Existing Conditions in Canaan

The Canaanite peoples had largely occupied the more fertile valleys of the land before the Israelites invaded. Their cities were strongly fortified, and their armies included battalions of chariots. The valleys were desirable because they contained all the trade routes and most of the available water in the land. During the seven-year conquest of the land under Joshua the cities were defeated, but many of them were re-occupied by Canaanite peoples and remained as enemy strongholds during most of the period of the judges.

The Place and Purpose of Judges in Bible History

The book of Judges looks historically in two directions. First, it looks back to the victories and leadership of God's servant Joshua. Thus it begins with, "After the death of Joshua ..." (1:1). Second, it looks forward to the establishment of the kingdom and ends with, "In those days there was no king in Israel" (21:25). In the period between these times God intended that the twelve tribes complete the takeover and occupation of their assigned tribal areas. They were commanded to drive out or destroy the remaining Canaanites and to occupy their cities and farmlands. Most importantly, they were to maintain their unity under God by obeying God's law and by faithfully worshiping God through the priesthood and the tabernacle. These instructions had been given to them through Moses at Mount Sinai in the wilderness. They were repeated forty years later by Moses at Mount Nebo, and again by Joshua at the end of his life. God not only gave them this responsibility—but He also promised them victory if they would obey Him. But they failed to do that. They did not drive out the enemy, but instead lived alongside them and intermarried with them. They did not remove all the pagan idols and altars, but rather adopted the idolatry and immorality of the Canaanites. Because of these things, God disciplined them through oppression by their enemies. When they repented, He delivered them by means of the judges that He raised up.

God promised Israel victory if they would obey Him. But they failed to do that.

The writer, under the inspiration of the divine Author, the Holy Spirit, seems to have had a threefold purpose in recording this sad history:

- To demonstrate the effects of a godless culture on His people.
- To explain the necessity for God's judgment on those who compromised His holy standards.
- To show that God was faithful to His covenant with His chosen people, even though they sinned.

An Outline of the Book

The book of Judges divides easily into three sections. The first provides an introduction to the book and to the days in question. The second (the main part of the book) is a documentary of the deeds of the judges. The third is an appendix, which gives two illustrations of the depravity in the times of the judges.

1. The Background to the Days of the Judges (1:1–2:5)
2. The Documentary of the Deeds of the Judges (2:6–16:31)
3. Two Illustrations of the Depravity in the Times of the Judges (17:1–21:25)

The Oppressors and Judges of Israel

Oppressors	Judges	Passages	Years as Judge
1. Arameans	Othniel	Judges 3:7-11	40
2. Moabites	Ehud	Judges 3:12-30	80
3. Philistines	Shamgar	Judges 3:31	?
4. Canaanites	Deborah	Judges 4-5	40
5. Midianites	Gideon	Judges 6-8	40
	Tola	Judges 10:1-2	23
	Jair	Judges 10:3-5	22
6. Ammonites	Jephthah	Judges 10:6-12:7	6
	Ibzan	Judges 12:8-10	7
	Elon	Judges 12:11-12	10
	Abdon	Judges 12:13-15	8
7. Philistines	Samson	Judges 13-16	20

The Incomplete Conquest of Canaan

The first chapter identifies the problem that the tribes of Israel faced as they lived in a culture permeated with evil and under God's judgment. The problem is that they compromised their sworn promise to God made in the days of Moses and Joshua. They promised when God brought them into Canaan they would do everything He had commanded them. Their promises included the complete destruction of the Canaanite peoples and every vestige of their idolatry. They promised not to intermarry with them or join with them in any way. The conquest started out well under Joshua, but as time went on they failed in all these areas. Thus they compromised their ownership of the land, their relationship with the Canaanites, and their worship of the true God. Their compromise was a result of their lack of faith and their unwillingness to obey God.

After the Death of Joshua

The fact of Joshua's death is significant for the theme of Judges because no national leader replaced him. Each tribe was to fully possess and defend its assigned territory. This began while Joshua was still alive and continued after his death. Some of the incidents recorded in the first chapter took place before Joshua's death, and others took place after it. They are not arranged in chronological order, but rather in a geographical order from the center of the land, to the south, and then to the north. The tribes mentioned were the 9½ tribes who had inheritances on the west bank of the Jordan River.

Judah Possesses Its Inheritance (1:1-20)

When Joshua finished the national campaign, all the tribal leaders met at the base camp in Gilgal to arrange the boundaries of each tribe's inheritance. Later, when Joshua died, they met again to plan an orderly takeover of the allotted areas. It would involve a military advance followed by the civilian occupation of towns and farms. They evidently met in Shiloh where the tabernacle was and asked the Lord which tribe should be first to "go up for us against the Canaanites" (v. 1). God's answer was that Judah was to be the first. He said, "I have delivered the land into his hand" (v. 2). What follows to verse 21 reports the victories that the tribe of Judah won in their section of the land. Nearly three hundred years before this, Jacob had prophesied that Judah's hand would be "on the neck of their enemies" (Gen. 49:8). Jacob's prophecy would now be fulfilled. Judah's territory extended south from Jerusalem to Kadesh Barnea. Judah had the largest of all the tribal territories.

The people of the tribe of Judah then asked Simeon to join with them in taking over the cities from the Canaanites (v. 3). It made sense as Simeon was the smallest tribe and their allotment was limited to a number of towns within the borders of Judah (Josh. 19:1). Judah's proposal also showed their brotherly love and unity in taking over their God-given possessions. Simeon readily agreed. There is a lesson for us here in the guidance of God from *the general* to *the particular*. First, the people of Judah knew from the law given to Moses the location of their inheritance in the land (Joshua 15). Then, as a result of prayer, they received the order that they would be first to go (v. 2). Finally, they used some sanctified common sense, asking Simeon to join them to share the campaign and the victories.

Israel compromised their sworn promise to God made in the days of Moses and Joshua.

The principle illustrated here can be applied to the Christian who possesses his or her spiritual inheritance that has been won by Jesus Christ, our greater Joshua. The name Joshua in Hebrew is the equivalent of Jesus in English. Believers, like the Israelites, have obtained an inheritance in Christ (Eph. 1:11-13). We know the boundaries of our inheritance and we are guaranteed victory. But we will only enjoy it if we move into it, *possess it,* and make it our own. When we do this we too will face resistance from our enemy as the Israelites did. But knowing the certainty of victory should ensure we do not fail to obey our Commander.

The Victories at Bezek and Jerusalem (1:4-8)

The campaign of Judah to possess its inheritance can be divided by two phrases in the text. First, "Judah went up," presumably from the base camp, Gilgal, in the Jordan valley, to Jerusalem, in the hill country. And second, "Judah went down" from Jerusalem to the dry country in the south, and from there, to the lowlands toward the sea (v. 9). First there was a great victory at a fortified city named Bezek, where ten thousand were killed. The location of Bezek is not known, but it must have been somewhere near Jerusalem. Adoni-Bezek means *Lord of Bezek* and refers to the ruler of the city. The men of Judah pursued him, caught him, and cut off his thumbs and big toes to humiliate him and to render him unable to fight. When they did this he admitted that he deserved this kind of punishment from God because he had done the same thing to seventy other city rulers. It is remarkable that Adoni-Bezek, a pagan king, admitted that God had justly repaid him.

We will only enjoy our inheritance if we move into it, possess it, and make it our own.

This was a great victory for Judah, but it is marred by what Judah's leaders did to Adoni Bezek. They disobeyed God's clear instruction by mutilating the king rather than killing him (Deut. 7:1-2). They chose a Canaanite form of punishment. Their disobedience to God and their decision to follow pagan ways of the Canaanites were both indicators of their future failure to completely obey God.

The next battle for the men of Judah was against Jerusalem. They took the city, killed its people, and set it on fire (v. 8). It appears from our text that this occurred shortly after the destruction of Bezek, although the historical order of events is uncertain. Probably the army of Judah took the southern hill of the city at that time. But evidently they failed to occupy it, and the Jebusites re-occupied it. It was attacked later by the Benjamites, who did not drive out the Jebusites but instead lived among them (v. 21). The Jebusites held it until the time of David, when he captured it (2 Sam. 5:6-9). Jerusalem was on the border of Judah and Benjamin. Both tribes failed to drive out the Jebusites permanently during that time (cf. v. 21).

Victories in the South and the West (1:9-20)

From going *up* (v. 4), the men of Judah and Simeon now went *down* from Jerusalem southward and westward (v. 9). Their campaign in taking control of their allotments was conducted in phases: first, in the "mountains" or hill country (v. 9), then in the dry south or Negev (v. 16), and finally to the "lowland" between the hill country and the coastal plains (v. 19).

They began this phase with the battle for Hebron, nineteen miles south of Jerusalem. The account given here in verses 10 to 15 is largely repeated from Joshua 15:13-19. The reason for the repetition in the context of Judges probably has to do with the part Caleb played. He was one of the best known men of Judah during that period. His courageous faith in God illustrates that the most difficult fortress in the land, defended by the most fearsome giants, could be defeated. That model would inspire the soldiers of every tribe to follow his example.

Caleb had been one of the two faithful Israelite spies who believed Canaan could be conquered when ten others did not (Num. 13:6, 30). In this incident God gave him the privilege of personally capturing Hebron, which the ten unfaithful spies said could not be done, even by the entire army of the Israelites (Josh. 14:6-15). It is notable that the names of three famous giants are repeated here to remind us of the significance of the capture (v. 10).

Othniel proved himself to be a man who believed God and who acted on his belief.

The next city to be taken was Debir, eleven miles south of Hebron. It was formerly known as Kirjath Sepher. Caleb put out a challenge to the men of Judah that the one who successfully led the charge against Debir would be given his daughter Achsah as his wife. Othniel, the son of Caleb's younger brother, took up the challenge. He defeated the city and obtained Achsah as his wife, along with a parcel of land in the south that was without any spring of water. Achsah asked her father for a blessing, specifically, a field with springs of water. He granted her request with a field with both upper and lower springs. The reason for the details about Othniel, the hero of the capture of the city of Debir, is that Othniel became the first judge of Israel (3:9). He proved himself to be a man who believed God and who acted on his belief.

The Settlement of the South by Judah (1:16-20)

Arad was south of Hebron and one of the strongest cities in the Negev. Here we learn that instead of conquering it, the descendants of Judah joined with the descendants of Moses' father-in-law, called a "Kenite" here and a "Midianite" in the book of Exodus. They were Gentiles. Moses had invited them to accompany the Israelites to the Promised Land (Num. 10:29-32). Presumably they had been waiting in Gilgal for a place to settle. Now they joined the people of Judah and settled in the Negev near Arad where they "dwelt among the people." These too fell short of God's command to destroy them. Their action—or lack of it—was compromise.

Next, Judah together with the Simeonites attacked the city of Zephath and destroyed it. Then they renamed it Hormah, meaning total destruction (v. 17). From there the army of Judah moved eastward to the coastal lowlands, where they took three cities, Gaza, Ashkelon, and Ekron (v. 19). The entire maneuver is summarized with two positive statements and one caveat. The first is that "the Lord was with Judah." It means that as they trusted Him, and were obedient, He gave them victory after victory. However, they could not hold the cities they captured, for very soon these same cities were listed as unconquered (3:5). The second positive statement was that they "took possession of the hill country." The hill country is the spine of hills that runs north and south through the center of the country.

Dealing with Chariots

Then comes the caveat: but they "could not drive out the inhabitants of the plain because they had chariots of iron" (v. 19). The Canaanites at that time were beginning to master the technology of smelting and using iron. The chariots operated well in the level valleys and were more than a military match for the Israelite foot soldiers. But the chariots could not be effectively used in the rugged terrain of the hill country. The problem for the men of Judah was not the superiority of the enemy's fearsome weapons. Their real problem was their lack of faith in God. Their fathers had seen God destroy Pharaoh's six hundred chariots in the Red Sea. Their leaders, Moses and Joshua, had both promised them that enemy chariots would pose no problem if they trusted in God (Deut. 20:1; Josh. 17:16-18). Their children would witness Judge Deborah defeat nine hundred chariots (4:13-16). In short, *their fear*

Judah won a great series of victories by trusting God.

had overcome their faith. In a final note the author reminds us that Judah's key accomplishment in the whole campaign was the capture of Hebron by Caleb, who drove out the three sons of Anak the giant (v. 20). Judah won a great series of victories by trusting God, but the victories were mostly compromised by failures to obey all that God had commanded them.

Incomplete Obedience (1:21-36)

The rest of the chapter is a continuation of compromise begun by Judah in the south. It shows the inability of the other tribes on the west bank of the Jordan to gain control of the territories from Jerusalem northward. Although Judah had previously captured Jerusalem (v. 8), the Jebusites had resumed their control of the city. Now Benjamin also tried and failed to drive the Jebusites out of Jerusalem. Instead of capturing it they settled down in a state of compromise alongside the Jebusites (v. 21).

After Benjamin, "Joseph" is mentioned next. The inheritance of Joseph had been divided into two tribes named after his two sons, Ephraim and Manasseh. Both tribes seem to be involved here as it is called "the house of Joseph." They attacked the prominent city of Bethel, and it says, "The LORD was with them." Spies had obtained information from a resident about a secret entrance, perhaps a tunnel, into the city. The spies offered him and his family "mercy," a covenant term, so that when the city was captured they were allowed to escape to the "land of the Hittites," where they built a similar city with the same name, Luz. But again there was compromise in that the spies made a covenant with the enemy. They had disobeyed God's clear command to utterly destroy the cities (Deut. 7:2).

Manasseh's territory included five important cities of the plain of Jezreel. Two of them, Beth Shean and Megiddo, controlled the great road from Egypt to Mesopotamia. But instead of driving out the inhabitants, Manasseh only forced them to pay tribute (vv. 27-28). In the southwest corner of Ephraim's territory was the strategically placed city of Gezer, but Ephraim allowed the Canaanites to live in it (v. 29). Zebulun also failed when they only demanded tribute from two cities (v. 30).

Asher also failed to drive out the Canaanites from seven cities (vv. 31-32). Instead, the people of Asher moved in with them. Naphtali failed to drive out the Canaanites and lived with them (v. 33). Issachar is not mentioned by name, probably because there were no cities of note in their territory. They probably shared Naphtali's misfortunes in Galilee. The tribe of Dan failed to conquer the Amorites near the coast and was forced to live in the hills (v. 34). Many Danites moved north to upper Galilee (Josh. 19:47). Only later did the house of Joseph put the Danite cities under forced labor. The Amorites controlled much of the land from Akrabim, south of the Dead Sea all the way to the north (v. 36). Thus all of the 9½ tribes with allotted areas west of the Jordan compromised God's clear instructions to possess the land and to drive out the Canaanites. The first chapter of Judges sets the theme (for the whole book) of *failure through disobedience.*

The Lord's Message on the Broken Covenant (2:1-5)

After the dismal record of Israel's failure to trust God and fully occupy Canaan, God intervened with a somber message for the people of Israel. In it He reminds them of two great themes that are at the heart of the book of Judges. The first is that *God was faithful* in keeping His covenant. The second is that *His people were unfaithful* and broke His covenant. As an introduction to the message we learn of a highly symbolic act by the Angel of the Lord. The Angel of the Lord is not merely *an* angel from the Lord, but *the* Angel of the Lord. He is a divine Person who occasionally revealed Himself to people in Old Testament times, always on very special occasions and with an important message. He refers to Himself as God and is to be identified with the second Person of the Trinity, the Son of God, the Lord Jesus Christ. He appeared to Abraham (Gen. 22:15), to Moses (Ex. 3:2-25), to Gideon (6:11-24), and to others.

God was faithful in keeping His covenant. His people were unfaithful and broke His covenant.

From Gilgal to Bochim (2:1-2)

It is most significant on this occasion that the Angel of the Lord came from Gilgal. It was the place where the Israelites had first entered the land and renewed the sign of their covenant with God, that is, circumcision (Gen. 17:10-11; Josh. 5:2-5). Because of their obedience under Joshua, God gave them national victory over the Canaanites (cf. 2:7). In our passage, the Angel of the Lord departed from Gilgal and came to Bochim, where He delivered a message for the generation after Joshua.

In His speech the Angel reminded them of the covenant He made with Abraham (vv. 1-2). God promised to give Abraham three things. (1) He would give him descendants who would become a nation; (2) He would give that nation a land of their own; and (3) He would ultimately make them a blessing to the world. The Israelites were His covenant people. He had kept His covenant when He made a nation of them in Egypt and raised up Moses to lead the new nation out of Egypt. He kept His covenant when He gave the new nation His law on Mount Sinai and the means whereby they could approach Him in worship. He had kept His covenant when He brought them through the wilderness and when He gave them the land of Canaan. He did all this because He had promised that He would never break His covenant with them (v. 1b; Deut. 7:9). God was, is, and always will be true to His covenant with Israel.

God was, is, and always will be, true to His covenant with Israel.

Now at Bochim He confronted them with the command He had given them at Mount Sinai, "You shall make no covenant with them and their gods. They shall not dwell in your land, lest they make you sin against me; for if you serve their gods, it will surely be a snare to you" (Ex. 23:32-33; cf. Judg. 2:2). But they had not listened to the voice of God. They had disobeyed by making treaties with the Canaanites instead of destroying them. They had not torn down the Canaanite idols and altars. If they had obeyed, God's unlimited resources would have always been available to them (Deut. 28:2, 7-8). So God challenged them to explain it. "What is this you have done?" (that is, all that is recorded in chapter 1).

The Consequences of Compromise (2:3-5)

Without waiting for an answer the Angel then reminded them that because of their disobedience they would have to endure the consequences of their compromise with the Canaanites. It is a statement of God's faithfulness to past warnings (Josh. 23:13). God, therefore, would not drive their enemies out of the land. The Canaanites would be thorns in their sides, and their gods would be a snare to them. The Israelites thought the idols would bring them prosperity, but the truth was that by following their gods they would be caught like a fly in a spider's web (v. 3).

The congregation of Israelites wept when they heard of the just and inevitable consequences of their compromise and disobedience. Having been deeply moved by what the Angel said, they named the place Bochim (meaning: *weepers*). Then they offered sacrifices to the Lord. These outward actions showed that they were sorry for their actions, but did not seem to reflect genuine or lasting repentance.

Judges begins with a record of the Israelites' growing disobedience to God and their inability to possess and enjoy the inheritance that God had given them. They illustrate second-generation believers who know the blessing their parents have enjoyed, but are unwilling to trust God themselves or obey Him as they did. They want God's blessing but fail to enjoy it because they compromise their faith in Him and do not make their faith a first-hand experience.

LESSON 1 EXAM

Use the answer sheet that has been provided to complete your exam.

1. **The book of Judges records the history of Israel**
   A. from Israel's entrance into the Promised Land until the death of Joshua.
   B. from the death of Joshua to just prior to the establishment of the kingdom.
   C. from the establishment of the kingdom to the death of David.
   D. from the exodus of Israel from Egypt to their entrance into the Promised Land.

2. **Which word best describes the main sphere of activity of the judges?**
   A. Judicial
   B. Religious
   C. Military
   D. Organizational

3. **The history of the Israelites' relationship with God during this period is recorded in a series of __________ cycles of disobedience, departure, discipline, and deliverance.**
   A. 7
   B. 10
   C. 12
   D. 20

4. **The period of the judges lasted for over**
   A. 100 years.
   B. 200 years.
   C. 300 years.
   D. 500 years.

5. **Because of the Israelites' disobedience, God**
   A. disciplined them through oppression by their enemies.
   B. cancelled His covenant with them.
   C. chose the descendants of Joshua to be His people.
   D. lowered His requirements to allow for their behavior.

6. **How many sections does the book divide into?**
   A. 3
   B. 4
   C. 5
   D. 6

7. **The problems the Israelites confronted as they lived in Canaan were caused by**
   A. the overwhelming strength of the Canaanites.
   B. the fact that they had compromised their sworn promise to God.
   C. conflict among the tribes.
   D. the difficult terrain of the land.

8. **Judah's victory at Bezek and the humiliation of King Adoni-Bezek was marred by**
   A. the number of fatalities in the battle.
   B. the insignificant location of the city.
   C. the attitude of Adoni Bezek.
   D. the disobedience of the Israelites.

9. **Caleb's courageous faith in God illustrates that**
   A. we do not have to fight for what God has promised us.
   B. the most difficult situations can be defeated.
   C. it takes a large army to defeat the enemy.
   D. life is easy for those who trust God.

10. **The response of the Israelites to the angel's message about the consequences of their actions demonstrated**
   A. sorrow for their disobedience.
   B. genuine and lasting repentance.
   C. resistance to God's discipline.
   D. disinterest in God's leadership.

What Do You Say?

What effect has the sin of compromise had in your Christian life?

LESSON 2

The Downward Spiral

Judges 2:6–3:6

Changes after the Death of Joshua (2:6-10)

In this section there is a second introduction—this time, a *theological explanation* of what would happen during the time of the judges. We learn of ...

- the new generation who did not know God.
- the departure of the Israelites away from God.
- the gracious acts of God in sending judges to deliver them from their enemies.
- the consequences of breaking their covenant with God.
- God's purpose in allowing the nations to remain in Canaan.

As with the *historical introduction* in chapter 1, this section begins with a link to the death of Joshua. Shortly before he died, Joshua had gathered the Israelites at Shechem and led them in a promise to remain faithful to the Lord (Joshua 24). Joshua reviewed the history of their ancestors from the time God made a covenant with Abraham until the present. Joshua went on to declare that he and his house would serve the Lord no matter what happened. The Israelites of all twelve tribes renewed their promise not to forsake the Lord. They declared, "We also will serve the LORD." They meant that they would destroy the Canaanites and their gods, possess all the land that had been given to them, and worship only Yahweh as He had instructed Moses at Mount Sinai.

Then Joshua warned them that God would judge them if they did not keep their promise. Once again they answered that they would serve the Lord (Josh. 24:18, 21). Notice that the phrases in verses 6 to 9 of our passage are almost identical to those in Joshua 24:28-31. Nothing could have been clearer to the people than their responsibility to possess the land in God's way. They fully understood their declaration that they would obey the Lord completely. Then each tribe went to its inheritance intending to destroy the remaining Canaanites and the pagan altars. For the next few years they "served the LORD" until the deaths of Joshua and the elders who outlived him (cf. Josh. 24:31). It seems probable that the visit of the Angel to Bochim was before Joshua actually died, for it was Joshua who dismissed the people (v. 6).

The "book of the law" was central in Joshua's life.

Joshua's leadership was an important key to the response of the people (v. 7). As a leader he ranks among the greatest in the whole Bible. Two things stand out from the beginning about his leadership. First, the *"Book of the law"* was central in his life from the time that God placed him in leadership (Josh. 1:8). He made it his own by meditating on what God had commanded. He shared it with others by teaching it, and he obeyed its commands.

The second thing that stands out is his *faith in God*. Because he believed the promises of God, he led the whole nation across the flooded Jordan River, marched around Jericho, and enjoyed their first military victory in the land. Since that time he had commanded the Israelites in victory after victory against overwhelming odds—all by faith. God used Joshua because he trusted in Him.

The Influence of Joshua in His Generation

Joshua's leadership made a huge difference to the people he was leading, so they willingly served the Lord as long as he lived. What a difference one person can make for good in the lives of others! Every one of us can make a significant difference to those around us. The opportunity is limited to our lifetime, so let's not miss it. Joshua died at age 110 and was buried at Timnath Heres in his own land in the tribal area of Ephraim. Within a few years the generation that conquered the land with Joshua was gone and a new generation arose (v. 10).

In the plan of God, Joshua had not arranged for a successor to take his place. God wanted the Israelites to focus on serving Him directly rather than on following a human ruler. They began well, but after Joshua's death their memories of Yahweh's great works began to fade, their service to Him declined, and their victories turned to defeats. They knew God had promised them the land unconditionally. And they supposed that God would let them do what they wanted there. Somehow they thought they could take care of themselves. In their growing unbelief they did not acknowledge the Lord's grace in giving them the land, nor did they accept any responsibility to Him.

The Failure of the People in the Next Generation (2:10)

"And there arose another generation ... who did not know the LORD or the work that he had done for Israel." These sad words introduce us to the pattern of the book of Judges. The second generation was marked out by its faithlessness. When it says that they did not know the Lord or His works, it does not mean that they had no information about Him or about His mighty acts. As children, some of them had crossed the Jordan and witnessed the soldiers marching around Jericho. As adults they had affirmed the words of Joshua that they would serve the Lord. Not knowing the Lord meant that they did not know Him experientially. They had no place for the Lord in their present lives or in their future plans.

Some writers call this the "Second Generation Syndrome," where the spiritual excitement of the first generation is succeeded by apathy and complacency in the second. The reality of their parents' faith had become merely stories that were not relevant to them. God no longer had priority in their day-to-day existence (Rev. 2:4; 3:16). It is part of a pattern that has always beset God's people. Second-generation believers often know *about* the truth, but their knowledge is merely intellectual understanding and not a living experience; it is a secondhand experience. How many have grown up in fine Christian homes, and then as young adults have turned their backs on the relevance of Christian truth!

Not knowing the Lord meant that they did not know Him experientially.

And how does it happen? Slowly, almost imperceptibly, the first-generation leaders grow old and die (2:10). Those who follow them have accepted as normal the stability that the first generation accomplished, but have not embraced the power of God in their lives. However, the pressures of life remain when the first generation has gone. But without the reality of God's presence, the visionary leadership and strong faith in God to face the pressure is gone. These second-generation believers are already on the path of compromise, and the path of least resistance is always downward.

The Downward Spiral in the Times of the Judges (2:11-15)

These verses form a preview of the downward spiral of Israel's relationship with the Lord during the next 340 years. Look at them in bullet form and notice the downward progression.

- They did not know the Lord (v. 10).
- They did evil in the sight of the Lord (v. 11).
- They forsook the Lord (vv. 12-13).
- They provoked the anger of the Lord (v. 14).
- The hand of the Lord was against them (v. 15).
- They experienced great distress (v. 15).
- The Lord raised up judges who delivered them (v. 16).
- When the judges were dead, they turned aside from the Lord again (v. 17).

There were seven of these cycles in a downward spiral, each sinking deeper than the one before. And each of these cycles must be understood in light of the fact that all those who rejected God had seen Him deliver His people from the previous cycle. In other words, they deliberately shut God out of their reasoning.

Rebellion (2:11-13)

The phrase "And the people of Israel did what was evil in the sight of the Lord" is used six times in Judges (v. 11; 3:7, 12; 4:1; 6:1; 10:6). The Hebrew reads that the evil they did was actually the *supreme evil.* And more than that, it conveys that they threw themselves at it. That supreme evil was to turn away from the true God and to serve false gods. The Israelites forsook the Lord God of their fathers and embraced Baal. Baal was the storm (weather) god of the Canaanites. The plural "baals" refers to different idols representing the same god, not to more than one god. The word "Baal" is a title meaning "lord" and is used more than seventy times in the Bible. Baal's consort was Ashtoreth, the goddess of sensual love and war. Canaanite religion centered on these two gods, who represented the fertility of the ground and the fertility of the people.

The Canaanites expressed their devotion to these gods by "acts of sympathy," meaning that they worshipped by doing what their gods did. This meant that in their sacred places the Canaanites gave themselves to all sorts of sexual prostitution and drunken orgies. It was as depraved and degraded as any religious practice on earth. By the time the Israelites invaded Canaan, the iniquity of the people had reached the point where it was ripe for God's severe judgment and the destruction of all its people (cf. Gen. 15:16). The depravity of the Canaanites was not only evident in their religion, but also in their general morality, ethics, values, and lifestyles.

Adding Insult to Injury (2:13)

Think of it! The Lord's own chosen people were turning away from Him who is "majestic in holiness" (Ex. 15:11) and adopting the immoral, pagan, and depraved religious practice of the Canaanites. They had been given more opportunity to know Him and serve Him than anyone else on earth. But now they loved what God told them to hate, and they kept what God told them to destroy. How could this happen? How could they deliberately put aside God's grace when it was by grace He had rescued them from slavery, delivered them from Pharaoh, guided them in the wilderness, fed them, and given them water to drink and victory over their enemies? Then He gave them the land itself with its cities and farms. And now to add insult to injury, they adopted Baal and Ashtoreth as their gods and bowed down to them. So it is with believers today who allow their love to grow cold little by little until they are living in routine disobedience to God.

The phrase "The children of Israel did evil in the sight of the Lord" is used six times in Judges.

Retribution (2:14-15)

No wonder the anger of the Lord burned against Israel. God does not display His anger in a burst of emotion. His is a righteous and holy anger against acts of wickedness, and against the rejection of His grace. How angry He must be at people today who call themselves Christians, but who have left Him out of their lives and consistently disobey His commands. God's righteous anger against Israel was expressed in His retribution. " He gave them over to plunderers ... and He sold them into the hand of their surrounding enemies." Notice that it was God who orchestrated their plundering and defeat. He was "against them for harm." It happened just as

God had explained to Moses before they entered the land (Deut. 31:16-21). And because of the Lord's retribution on them they were in terrible distress.

Preview of Israel's Spiritual and Moral Decline (2:16-19)

In this section the writer explains the downward spiral of Israel as a preview of the whole period of the judges. Though repentance was usually part of the cycles, it is not specifically mentioned here, perhaps because their repentance was usually less than complete. It simply says that in their distress the Lord raised up judges to deliver them. And when the judges delivered them they would not listen, but instead played the harlot with the false gods (v. 17). The preview here does give a hint of their pain when it says that "the LORD was moved to pity by their groaning" because of those who "afflicted and oppressed them." And their pain is even more obvious five other times when it specifically says that they cried out to the Lord in their distress (3:9, 15; 4:3; 6:6; 10:10). Thus the pattern in Judges is clearly established. It begins with the people's *rebellion* and God's *retribution.* It ends with the people's *repentance* and God's *rescue.*

We should also keep in mind that the Lord was closely associated with the judges. Notice three things about the Lord's part in verse 18. First, *the judges were appointed by the Lord.* It was the Lord who raised them up. Second, *the judges were empowered by the Lord* to accomplish their task. Third, *the Lord used the judges* to deliver the people out of the hand of their enemies. The point is that the judges were God's agents. The people and their leaders were to be subjects of the Lord, not of the state. They had a minimum of human structured authority in government and a maximum of opportunity for people at all levels to be subject to God.

In His compassion, God raised up judges who delivered His people from their enemies.

In our study of the judges themselves we will note that there were six "major" judges whose leadership is given substantial treatment. These were Othniel, Ehud, Deborah, Barak, Gideon, and Jephthah. There were also six "minor" judges, minor in the sense that they receive only slight comment. They were Shamgar, Tola, Jair, Ibzan, Elon, and Abdon. Some of them rose to become national leaders while others remained tribal leaders. Sometimes more than one of them served at the same time.

Israel's Groaning and the Lord's Compassion (2:18-19)

God's response to Israel's groaning is an insight into the heart of God reaching out in grace. Their "groaning" because they were "oppressed" reminds us of their bondage under Pharaoh when they "groaned" because they were "oppressed" (Ex. 2:24; 6:5). But there is no mention in either situation of them crying out to Him. Then, in His compassion, God raised up judges who delivered them out of the hand of their enemies. But even when God provided a deliverer it did not cause the people to stop their "stubborn way." The word "stubborn" or stiff-necked was used of Israel when Aaron made the golden calf (Ex. 32:9; 33:3, 5). Their stubbornness continued throughout their history (Ps. 78:8ff).

The people never seemed to learn their lesson, and after the death of each judge their corruption not only continued, but increased (v. 19). The next generation behaved more corruptly in following the pagan gods than their fathers did. Thus the downward spiral continued and the cycles of rebellion, retribution, repentance, and rescue went on for 340 years. Verse 19 ends with a significant conclusion. "They did not drop any of their practices or their stubborn ways." Literally it reads, "They refused to drop any of their impious actions." So the pattern of evil not only repeated itself but also intensified as it descended downward. The commentator Daniel Block speaks of the "irresistible, irreversible, and inevitable process of Canaanization."

God's Anger because of the Broken Covenant (2:20-23)

The consequence was that God's anger was "kindled" against Israel. He said, "This people have transgressed My covenant" (cf. 2:12, 14). When He used the term "this people" instead of "My people" He expressed His alienation from it. He put Israel in the same category as the Canaanite "nations." In the first verse of this chapter God said that He would never break the covenant, but now *this* "people," Israel, had broken the covenant they made with Him (see 2:1, Ex. 19:5-8).

The Angel of the Lord commanded them not to make a covenant with the Canaanites. But they had disobeyed, as we clearly saw in chapter 1, where six times it says that one tribe after another did not drive out the Canaanites (1:27-33). So the Angel told them in 2:3 that *He* would not drive out the Canaanites. Now in His anger He reiterates that none of the nations which Joshua left when he died would be driven out. This will be confirmed in the remaining chapters of Judges; not one of the battles fought secured any more land for God's people.

We too can get swallowed up by the prevailing culture of the world and go further and further away from fellowship with God.

God's Discipline of Israel through the Canaanites (3:1-6)

This section deals with the identity of the unconquered nations and God's sovereign purpose for Israel in using them to discipline Israel. We have already learned that the Lord allowed the Canaanite nations to remain in the land for several reasons. First, to punish the disobedient Israelites. They would be like thorns in Israel's side because Israel had adopted the idol gods of Canaan instead of destroying them (2:3). Second, He allowed them to remain in order to "test" Israel's faithfulness to Him (2:22, 3:1, 4). Each new generation would be tested as to whether they obeyed God or disobeyed Him. Thus those who had not fought with Joshua would have their own opportunity to choose to serve God.

Each new generation would be tested as to whether they obeyed God or disobeyed Him.

A third reason why He allowed the Canaanites to stay in the land was to give Israel some experience in warfare so that when they faced the larger powers they would have experience. A final reason was to prevent the land from becoming a wilderness while the population of Israel was still relatively small (Ex. 23:29-30; Deut. 7:20-24). If these purposes seem somewhat contradictory, we must remind ourselves that the sovereign purposes of God often defy human logic.

Four of the Canaanite enemies are mentioned. First, the Philistines and their five lords near the southern coast. These would be Israel's main enemies for hundreds of years to come. The Sidonians were Phoenicians whose principal city was Sidon and later, Tyre. They dominated the northern coast. The Hivites dwelt in the north-central part of the land. Shechem and Gibeon were Hivite cities. The Hittites (v. 5) were a people whose empire was centered in Anatolia (modern Turkey). They also had strong settlements in Judah, such as in Hebron.

Three Steps to Spiritual Disaster (3:5-6)

The final verses summarize the progression of Israel's departure from God and their unity with the Canaanites. All three steps were in rebellious defiance of God's clearly understood commands. First they *lived among them*. Then they *intermarried with them*. Finally, they *served their gods*. These three steps spelled spiritual disaster.

The lessons in Israel's experience for alert believers today are clear. The danger of compromise with the world is as real now as it was then. We too can fall into disobedience to God. And if we rebel it will lead to God's discipline or painful correction. If, in our pain, we respond to God's discipline, then God graciously gives us opportunity to repent. And if we repent, then God may deliver us in His sovereign grace and give us another opportunity to live for Him—but how much better to reject the world and remain faithful to Him in the first place!

LESSON 2 EXAM

Use the answer sheet that has been provided to complete your exam.

1. **When Joshua challenged the people at Shechem to faithfully serve the Lord, they**
   A. were hesitant about making such a promise.
   B. promised they would obey the Lord completely.
   C. did not understand what he meant.
   D. gave half-hearted agreement.

2. **Joshua's __________ made him one of the greatest leaders recorded in Scripture.**
   A. military skill and his choice of leadership
   B. knowledge of people and his interpersonal skills
   C. organizational ability and his leadership style
   D. focus on the law of God and his faith in God

3. **Joshua did not arrange for a successor because**
   A. the tribes were so scattered.
   B. he didn't care what happened in the future generations.
   C. there was no one with the proper qualifications.
   D. God wanted Israel to serve Him directly.

4. **The next generation after Joshua's**
   A. followed the Lord whole-heartedly.
   B. did not know the Lord experientially.
   C. depended on the Lord's power.
   D. obeyed the Lord completely.

5. **The supreme evil that the Israelites committed was**
   A. turning away from the true God to serve false gods.
   B. intermarrying with other tribes.
   C. failing to possess their territory.
   D. returning to Egypt.

6. **The depraved Canaanite religion and lifestyle was centered on the gods**
   A. Molech and El.
   B. Baal and Ashtoreth.
   C. Jehovah and Baal.
   D. Chemosh and Jehovah.

7. **God's righteous anger prompted Him to**
   A. coax the Israelites to return to Him.
   B. totally destroy the Israelites.
   C. give Israel into the Canaanites' hands in retribution.
   D. turn His back on the Israelites.

8. **God's response to raise up judges for His people stemmed from**
   A. His anger.
   B. His compassion.
   C. the people's repentance.
   D. the people's demands.

9. **One of the things the angel of the Lord said to Israel was that**
   A. God was going to renew His covenant with them.
   B. all their existing enemies would become fearful of them.
   C. none of the nations left undefeated under Joshua would now be driven out.
   D. they would disappear as a nation.

10. **One of the reasons God allowed the Canaanites to stay in the land was**
    A. to test the faithfulness of each generation of Israelites.
    B. to give them another chance to turn to Him in repentance.
    C. to provide justice for all people.
    D. His compassion for their children.

What Do You Say?

Comment on the concept of "second-generation Christians" and how it can be guarded against.

LESSON 3

A Few Good Men in Bad Times

Judges 3:7-31

Examples of God's Faithfulness to His Covenant

The main section of the book now gives us seven examples of the fourfold pattern described in 2:7 to 3:6. The examples are not in chronological order, but rather in an order that develops the theme. They are arranged to emphasize the spiritual and moral decline of the Israelites and the resulting consequences.

During the whole period of 340 years, the Lord had a greater purpose than simply delivering His people out of trouble. As recorded in Genesis 12:1-3, He had made an unconditional covenant with Abraham to bless the whole world through his descendants (Deut. 9:4-6). He would honor His covenant for all time and through all circumstances. The covenant provided for the coming of a Redeemer-King who would defeat Satan, bring salvation to mankind, and eventually bring peace on earth. The book of Judges shows how this great purpose was being worked out in those times. God had reminded Israel in 2:1, "I will never break My covenant with you." Now in these central chapters we have some remarkable examples of how He honored His covenant.

The Example of Othniel (3:7-11)

The first example of the cycles that occurred during the judges' period presents a pattern; it helps us understand the ones that follow. Because of its brevity and simplicity as a pattern, it omits many details. The reader is meant to concentrate on the pattern of *disobedience, departure, discipline,* and *deliverance* that was introduced in the first two chapters. The pattern begins with the unfaithfulness of the Israelites, "did what was evil in the sight of the LORD. They forgot the LORD their God and served the Baals and the Asheroth," the idol gods of the Canaanites (v. 7).

God's response was to make them a vassal nation to a king from Mesopotamia named Cushan-rishathaim. The king's name is literally "Cushan–double wickedness." It may be a name describing his wicked character, such as the name of the Russian Czar "Ivan the Terrible." Or it may be a play on the Hebrew word for Mesopotamia in the same verse, which is "Aram-naharaim," which means "Aram of the double rivers." The pun then would indicate that Cushan was "double evil from the double rivers." Whoever he was, God allowed him to keep the Israelites in bondage for eight years (1381–1373 BC). Then the Israelites in their distress, "cried out to the LORD." It was not a cry of repentance, but one of misery. But even though they had not repented, the Lord had compassion on His people and responded to relieve them of their misery by raising up a deliverer whose name was Othniel.

God in His sovereignty controls the destinies of nations.

We have already been introduced to Othniel in the introduction to the book (1:11-15). Othniel was the younger half-brother of Caleb, a man of great faith and courage during the invasion of Canaan many years before. At that time Caleb had asked for the privilege of leading an attack against the heart of Canaanite power at Kiriath-arba, or Hebron. God gave him a great victory there (Josh. 15:13-19). But not many miles south of Hebron was another strong fortress called Kiriath Debir. Caleb offered his daughter Achsah in marriage to the one who captured it. Othniel accepted the challenge, captured Debir, and married Achsah.

Now it was years later. Othniel is the man God raised up to be the military commander who would defeat Cushan-rishathaim and free the Israelites from bondage. It is probable that in the intervening years the story of his skill and courage had spread to the northern part of the country, so when the people needed a military leader, it was Othniel who came to mind. When he called for those willing to follow him to war, he soon had an army. We do not have the details, but Cushan probably took the same route as the four invading kings in the days of Abraham (Genesis 14). Like them he came around the Fertile Crescent and approached the land of Israel from the north. Like them he would attack one city after another, looting and pillaging as he went. During that time, Othniel in Judah gathered his army. Then at some unknown location Othniel was able to engage Cushan in a battle and God delivered the army of Mesopotamia into his hand (v. 10). The main point is that it was God who did it through His servant.

The Character of the Lion

Othniel's name means "lion of God," and his character matched his name. He was a *man of skills* having proved he could handle weapons of war and lead others to victory. He was a *man of courage* and demonstrated it when he volunteered to face the giants at Kiriath-sepher. He was a *man of faith* in that he believed that the God who instructed him to go would be responsible to give him victory. And now he was a man who was *filled with the Spirit of the Lord.* The Spirit enabled him to raise an army and to lead it successfully against King Cushan of Mesopotamia. The Spirit directed him to call the Israelites back to the Lord so that they did not slip back into apostasy for forty years. Thus there was peace in Israel for an entire generation of people. Note the comment in the text that it was not the people but the land that had rest (v. 11).

The obvious lesson for us is that God is still looking for people of skill, courage, and faith who are filled with the Spirit of God and who will let God use them.

The Example of Ehud (3:12-30)

The second example of Israel's continued downward path toward becoming like the Canaanites follows the pattern set in the first one. Israel forgot the penalty for idolatry and again "did what was evil" with the result that the Lord allowed them to be overrun by an enemy. Then the Israelites cried to the Lord, and He in His mercy sent them a deliverer whose name was Ehud. The Lord enabled the deliverer to defeat the enemy and gave rest to the land once more.

Eglon, King of Moab

When Israel "did what was evil," the Lord strengthened Eglon, king of Moab, to invade Israel and subjugate its people. Moab was located east of the southern half of the Dead Sea. Moabites were descendants of Lot and perennial enemies of Israel. King Balak of Moab opposed the Israelites when they came from Egypt (Numbers 22–24). Now King Eglon became God's agent to discipline Israel for their apostasy. Moab was not even listed among the enemy nations of chapters 1 and 2, but God in His sovereignty controls the destinies of nations and this time He used Moab to do His work. King Eglon was able to enlist the help of both Ammon and Amalek to assist his army. Like the Moabites, the Ammonites were descendants of Lot. The Amalekites were wilderness-dwellers south of Judah.

With his army, Eglon came north along the east side of the Dead Sea and crossed the Jordan River at the fords near Jericho in much the same place as the Israelites had crossed many years before. Jericho was in the tribal territory of Benjamin. Eglon defeated the Israelites, who probably included warriors from Benjamin and Ephraim. He set up his base in the "city of palms," that is, Jericho. Earlier Joshua had invoked a curse on anyone who occupied that site, though Eglon may not have been aware of that (Josh. 6:26). He probably built his local administrative palace near to the ancient site and used the advantages of its excellent water supply, its good farmland, and its strategic access to Israel via the two valleys that lead from it to the heartlands of Benjamin and Ephraim. Eglon forced the Israelites to serve him and bring heavy tribute to him for eighteen long years (1334–1316 BC).

The Israelites Bring Tribute

Once again the Israelites "cried out to the LORD" (v. 15; cf. v. 9). And just as before, it was not a cry of repentance, but a cry of pain. In His compassion the Lord again responded by raising up a deliverer. He was a Benjamite named Ehud, the son of Gera. The author describes Ehud as being left-handed, or perhaps ambidextrous like many Benjamites (1 Chron. 12:2). His skill with his left hand would enable him to accomplish the dangerous scheme he was planning. Ehud was the leader of a group of Benjamites who were selected to carry the annual tribute to King Eglon in Jericho. The goods demanded as tribute were probably made up of foods and wines and would need many people to carry them. Very likely they had been collected at a central point and were then transported and presented to the enemy king.

To prepare for his scheme, Ehud made a short double-edged dagger with no hilt, or crosspiece. He strapped the dagger to the inside of his right thigh. In this way it would be entirely concealed under his flowing garments. No one would suspect he was armed (v. 16). Using the dagger as his weapon Ehud devised a clever plan by which he hoped to assassinate King Eglon when he led the tribute takers to Jericho. One other important detail given was that King Eglon was very fat (v. 17).

Ehud Carries Out His Plan

After delivering the tribute to the king, Ehud led his group home going west, up the valley toward Jebus (Jerusalem). That valley is called the Ascent of Adummim. They came to some well-known idols by the road at a place called Gilgal. These were most likely Canaanite idols that the Benjamites had come to accept. The place named "Gilgal" cannot be the site of Israel's first camp that was east of Jericho; it must have been somewhere west of Jericho on the way to the hill country. It may be the Gilgal mentioned in Joshua 15:7, which was on the border between Benjamin and Judah and north of the Ascent of Adummim. Wherever it was, Ehud dismissed his carriers there and he turned back alone to revisit King Eglon in Jericho.

We should discern the theme and purpose of the story.

When he arrived at the palace in Jericho, Ehud requested a private audience with the king saying that he had a "message" for him. The king agreed and dismissed his attendants. Then he brought Ehud to the room on the roof where a breeze might offer some relief (v. 19). Ehud came near to King Eglon in his upper chamber and told him that he had a "message" from God. The king still did not suspect any treachery and stood up in reverence, believing he would receive a divine oracle. As the king stood up (perhaps with some difficulty due to his weight), Ehud drew his dagger with his left hand and drove it powerfully into the king's belly until the handle was embedded. The king fell over dead in a pool of his refuse without uttering a word. Ehud then locked the door to delay the attendants from learning what happened and left quickly. He passed by the palace guards as if nothing had happened.

After he had gone, the attendees went up to the king, but found the door locked. They delayed going in supposing that he was attending to his bodily needs. When they finally suspected something was wrong they opened the door to find King Eglon dead on the floor. Ehud, in the mean time, had made his escape. He passed the idols and escaped to Seirah, a town in Benjamin (vv. 20-26).

Israel Delivered

Note that there is nothing in the story about Ehud's spiritual status. We don't know if he was a godly man or not. We only learn that God raised him up as a deliverer much as He had strengthened pagan King Eglon to attack Israel. God did not necessarily approve of the method Ehud used. He is not even described as "judging Israel," let alone that the Spirit of God came upon him. However, the enemy king was dead and Ehud had successfully completed an heroic act. In this way he earned the respect of the tribes of Benjamin and Ephraim. Having done that, he "sounded the trumpet in the hill country of Ephraim" (v. 27). That is, he summoned the people into battle. They recognized him as their military leader and followed him. He said to them, "Follow after me, for the LORD has given your enemies the Moabites into your hand."

This story is an example of God saving and preserving His people for their role in His covenant plan to bless the world.

Ehud and his army then went down to the Jordan, probably north of Jericho, and then seized the fords of Jordan. This maneuver effectively cut off an escape route across the Jordan for the Moabite army. They were thrown into confusion and in the ensuing battle ten thousand Moabites were slain. Not one escaped. After the victory over the Moabites the land had rest "for eighty years" (v. 30). It is the same phrase used after the victory of Othniel. Eighty years is about two generations (1316-1227 BC).

We can we learn some good lessons from Ehud.

- He was a man of courage. He figured out what he could do, even though it was a daring scheme. Then he put his life on the line to do it.
- He had great self-control in the carrying out of his scheme to assassinate King Eglon.
- He had the confidence of the people so that when he had taken the first step, they rose to follow him into war.
- Whatever the quality of his personal godliness, he certainly understood that God would give them the victory and he persuaded others to follow him.

There are also wrong ways to interpret this incident.

- Allegorize them, so Ehud's dagger becomes the sword of the Spirit. The story is *not* about using the Word of God for "discerning the thoughts and intentions of the heart" (Heb. 4:12).

- Moralize them, by saying that Ehud is a bad example, so don't be like him. The story is not about our moral guidance.
- Trivialize them, by speaking of the value of odd details such as "left-handed assassins."

What we *should* do is discern the theme and purpose of the story. In this case the theme is an example of God saving and preserving His people for their role in His covenant plan to bless the world. This example takes place when His people are imperfect, living in an imperfect society. And when sinful people in a godless world cry out to God, He hears them and responds by saving them. So when people are disobedient and dreadful things happen, or when we find ourselves trapped in a mess caused by our own bad decisions, we can take comfort that God is still there.

There are sad elements to this story, because Ehud was not an adequate savior. He could not change the people or remove the idolatry from their hearts. They were held in the clutches of sin. But all of us can cry out to God for help. And the saving grace of our nail-scarred Savior can certainly free us from our bondage.

Shamgar (3:31)

The third example of a deliverer in the time of the judges is Shamgar. A single verse provides all the information we have about this man. His name is thought to be foreign as his father's name, Anath, was the name of a Canaanite god. On this basis some have thought Shamgar might not have been an Israelite. From the weapon he used so skillfully, an ox goad, we can see that he was a herdsman of cattle or a farmer. He may have been a contemporary of Ehud's, because Ehud's death is mentioned after the report on Shamgar (4:1). He seems to have settled near the border of Philistia and Judah. Living there he could carry out his activity of killing Philistines with his ox goad. It may be that he attacked Philistine raiding parties which would periodically raid the cities of Judah.

Ox goads were eight to ten feet long with an iron tip on one end and a flattened chisel blade on the other. The point was to prod the oxen as they pulled a plow or wagon, and the blade was used to clean the plows.

During the normal course of his life as a farmer, Shamgar killed six hundred Philistines with his ox goad. Like Ehud, Shamgar used an unconventional weapon. He is an illustration of the New Testament principle the apostle Paul wrote of: "God chose what is weak in the world to shame the strong . . . God chose what is low and despised in the world . . . that no human being might boast in the presence of God" (1 Cor. 1:27-29).

The end result of his single-handed attacks was that "he delivered Israel." Like Ehud he is seen as a deliverer, not just a "ruler" in Israel. His skill and bravery seem to be outstanding. In her victory song Deborah mentions Shamgar for his heroism (5:6).

LESSON 3 EXAM

Use the answer sheet that has been provided to complete your exam.

1. **The examples of God's faithfulness to His covenant as listed in Judges are arranged**
   A. in chronological order.
   B. in random order.
   C. in an order that develops the theme.
   D. in order of importance.

2. **One of the main long-range purposes of God's covenant with Israel was**
   A. to keep the Gentiles from obtaining blessing.
   B. to judge the world through them.
   C. to record world history.
   D. to provide through them a redeemer from sin.

3. **The pattern of the cycles as given in Judges 3:7 begins with**
   A. the unfaithfulness of the Israelites.
   B. God's judgment on the Israelites.
   C. the raising up of the first judge.
   D. the return of the Israelites to Jehovah.

4. **When the Israelites cried out under the oppression of Cushan-rishathaim it was**
   A. a cry of repentance.
   B. a cry of misery.
   C. a cry for a deliverer.
   D. a cry of anger.

5. **Othniel sets us the example of God using a man who had**
   A. courage, faith, and skill.
   B. personality and persuasiveness.
   C. neither A or B.
   D. both A and B.

6. **King Eglon of __________ was used by God to discipline the Israelites.**
   A. Amon
   B. Amalek
   C. Moab
   D. Philistia

7. **When the Israelites cried out to the Lord under the oppression of Eglon, the Lord raised up Ehud who was**
   A. a right-handed Benjamite.
   B. a left-handed Judahite.
   C. a left-handed Benjamite.
   D. a right-handed Judahite.

8. **In order to gain privacy to assassinate Eglon, Ehud**
   A. murdered his servants.
   B. hid in the bushes.
   C. created a diversion.
   D. told him he had a message from God.

9. **From the biblical account we discern that Ehud was a man of**
   A. godliness and spirituality.
   B. timidity and fear.
   C. courage and self-control.
   D. dissipation and carelessness.

10. **Shamgar killed 600 Philistines with**
   A. an ox-goad.
   B. a donkey's jawbone.
   C. a sword.
   D. a mill stone.

What Do You Say?

Of the three judges covered in this lesson, which one is an example to you right now, and how?

LESSON 4

A Prophetess in Dangerous Times

Judges 4:1–5:31

In Judges 4 and 5 we come to the fourth example of God's faithfulness in saving His people from the consequences of their own sin. Again the narrative follows the pattern of disobedience, departure, discipline, and deliverance. The departure is always the same, "And the people of Israel again did what was evil in the sight of the Lord" (v. 1). The first three oppressors had been foreign kings (from Mesopotamia, Moab, and Philistia). This time the oppressors were a coalition of kings from inside Canaan led by Jabin, king of Hazor, in the tribal area of Naphtali northwest of the Sea of Galilee. It was an important city in northern Israel on the main trade route between Egypt and Mesopotamia. Many years earlier, Joshua had destroyed and burned the city in obedience to God (Josh. 11:1-11).

Israel Backslides Again (4:1)

During Ehud's life and probably that of Shamgar the land had eighty years of rest. After their restraining influence against evil was gone, the Israelites again "did evil." Their "evil" was in exchanging the true worship of Yahweh for the sensual, corrupt, depraved worship of Canaanite gods. As their evil increased, little by little the city of Hazor was being rebuilt and fortified, like many other cities that Joshua had destroyed. The compromising Israelites did not seem to realize the increasing threat to their safety while the city walls were being rebuilt and the iron was being smelted for the chariots.

King Jabin and General Sisera (4:2-3)

King Jabin's name is the same as that of another king in Hazor whom Joshua defeated 150 years earlier. Jabin's Canaanite coalition army had a commander named Sisera, whose military base was in Harosheth Hagoyim. It means "Harosheth of the Gentiles" and is probably to be identified with Tell el-Harbaj near Mount Carmel. There Sisera commanded nine hundred iron-plated chariots as an attack force in his powerful army. With the chariots he could command and control the entire Plain of Esdraelon, also called the Valley of Jezreel, from Mount Carmel to the Sea of Galilee. On the plains, chariots were feared like modern tanks. The Israelites had no defense against them. Then Sisera attacked them and brought all of Galilee and northern Israel into submission and heavy oppression from King Jabin (vv. 2-3).

The Israelites learned by experience the principle that everyone who commits sin is a slave of sin.

The text explains that this was God's punitive action because they had been unfaithful to Him. It says, "And the LORD sold them" to another master, that is, to Jabin, king of Canaan (cf. 2:14; 3:8; 1 Sam. 12:9). And then it says that their new master, King Jabin, "harshly oppressed" them. Being out-gunned and out-manned they could only submit to the oppression of bondage and high taxes. It went on for twenty years. At that point, they "cried out to the LORD." They learned by experience the principle that everyone who commits sin is a slave of sin (John 8:34).

As previously mentioned, Jabin's re-emergence as a malign power after the first Jabin had been destroyed is an apt illustration of the resurgence of the strongholds of sin in our lives after past victories. It usually happens little by little so that we hardly notice our own spiritual decline.

Deborah the Prophetess (4:4-5)

It was when the Israelites came to realize the growing oppression of the Canaanites that we are introduced to Deborah. She was a prophetess and highly respected in Israel. Her home was between the towns of Ramah and Bethel in the hill country of Ephraim where she lived with her husband, Lapidoth. Because she was known as a prophetess the sons of Israel came to her for judgment. Many commentators have assumed that she was holding court on personal issues. But it is better to see that as a prophet of the Lord she was giving them His answer to the cries of the people over the harsh oppression by King Jabin. Deborah's "judgments" were not about civil disputes but about what God wanted the Israelites to do in their national crisis. She describes the severity of the crisis in her poem: "Jael, the highways were abandoned, and travelers kept to the byways. The villagers ceased ... until I arose ... a mother in Israel" (5:6-7). The fact that they came to her about their plight, rather than to the priests in nearby Shiloh near Bethel, probably indicates the low spiritual condition of the priests.

Deborah's role as a prophetess was outside the usual role of women in the Old Testament, but there were several other exceptions. She was like Miriam before her during the time of the exodus (Ex. 15:20), and like Huldah after her (2 Kings 22:14). Prophets were people who received a revelation from God in order to communicate it to people. Sometimes they spoke of God's will for the present and at other times of His will for the future. God specifically chose to work through Deborah by telling her what she was to do in this national crisis. She is the only woman in the Bible who was called by God to be a national leader.

Barak Called to Fight the Canaanites (4:6-7)

God told Deborah what to do. She was to mobilize 10,000 troops from the tribes of Zebulun and Naphtali and deploy them at Mount Tabor in the Valley of Jezreel. Mount Tabor was an unmistakable cone-shaped mountain rising 1,300 feet from the floor of the Valley of Jezreel. Deborah immediately summoned Barak to come fifty miles from his home in Kedesh to hers near Bethel. He was an experienced army commander and no doubt respected her as a prophet of God. When he came she told him of the Lord's calling, His strategy, and His victory. The Lord was calling them to action. He gave them the strategy of mobilizing ten thousand troops and deploying them to Mount Carmel. Finally, He promised the victory. He would defeat their enemy, Sisera.

Deborah's Prophecy (4:8-9)

Barak quickly agreed to go, but only if Deborah would go with him (v. 8). If he was hesitating, he had good biblical company—think of Moses and Jeremiah! (Ex. 4:13; Jer. 1:6). Many preachers and writers have taken his hesitation to mean that Barak was a weak and fearful man. But the Bible does not portray him like that. It cites Barak in God's "Hall of Fame" of the faithful (Heb. 11:32). He believed, against all the evidence to the contrary, that God would do exactly as He had promised.

Barak objected to going alone, however, and insisted on Deborah's presence. She represented God's presence in the battle which would guarantee victory. She was quick to say, "I will surely go with you." But she answers his objection by giving him a sign. The sign would be that when he saw the credit for the victory over Sisera going to a woman instead of him, he would know that he had been called by God. He probably thought, as we the readers do, that the woman who would receive the glory would be Deborah. That would come later. Deborah then rose up from her prophetic chair and went with Barak.

Barak and Deborah went to Kedesh, his home town near the southeast coast of the Sea of Galilee. From there Barak put out a call for men of Zebulun and Naphtali to report for military duty. Ten thousand men came. Barak trained them as a fighting force and they all moved north to Mount Tabor where they set up their camp as God had commanded. And Deborah went with him.

Heber the Kenite (4:10-16)

Then there is a curious parenthetical note in verse 11 about a descendant of Hobab (also called Jethro in Exodus 3:1), Moses' father-in-law. Hobab and his family came with Moses and the Israelites to Canaan and settled near Arad in southern Judah (1:16). But one of them, by name of Heber, had moved north from there with his family and settled near a famous tree beside Kedesh. It is most likely Kedesh Naphtali near the Sea of Galilee where Barak lived, although another Kedesh near Hazor remains a possibility. It is not surprising that as a foreigner Heber established good political relations with King Jabin (see v. 17). This is not just geographic trivia. It is inserted here because Heber's wife was Jael, who will play an important role in the story. God arranged for her to be there at the right place at the right time to perform her role as a sign to Barak.

Deborah is the only woman in the Bible who was called by God to be a national leader.

Meanwhile it was reported to Sisera, perhaps by Heber, that there were 10,000 Israelite troops assembled at Mount Tabor. Sisera responded immediately by mobilizing his army with all nine hundred chariots to the River Kishon just below Mount Tabor. When Sisera's army camped at the foot of the mountain, Deborah the prophetess, speaking for God, then said to Barak, "Up! For this is the day … Does not the LORD go out before you?" (v. 14). Deborah's role is finished at this point, and even Barak's role is diminished. The Lord was going before him and his troops. Humanly speaking it was a foolish military strategy. Barak left a place of strength on the mountain to fight against a vastly superior force on the plain where they could use their chariots with devastating effect. Sisera no doubt thought everything was in his favor.

But it was the Lord's battle, not Barak's. Barak simply believed the word of God through His prophetess Deborah and obeyed. It was the Lord who "routed Sisera … before Barak by the edge of the sword" (v. 15). The sword is now in the Lord's hand and all the action is "before" Barak (twice, vv. 14-15). The Lord was the warrior leading the battle.

Then the Lord did exactly what He promised He would do. It was at Taanach where "And the LORD routed Sisera and all his chariots and all his army" (cf. 5:19). What was left of the Canaanite army ran for their base in Harosheth. Even General Sisera saw the situation was hopeless and left his chariot, running away on foot. Barak and the Israelites chased the army and destroyed them all.

The Assassination of Sisera (4:17-22)

The story returns to Sisera on the run. He ran northeast from the Kishon battlefield at Taanach seeking refuge in the camp of his friend Heber with whom he had made some sort of peace treaty (v. 17). Heber's wife Jael was there. She offered him refuge and told him not to fear. He came into her tent with her assurance of safety and she further hid him by covering him with a blanket. Sisera then asked for a drink of water and she gave him milk, or possibly yogurt. He told her to stand at the door and if anyone asked she was to deny that there was any man there. Sisera was exhausted and soon fell into a deep sleep. Jael then approached him with a hammer and tent peg and quickly drove the tent peg through his temple and into the ground, killing him instantly (v. 21).

The story ends with the re-appearance of Barak, whom we last saw leading his army to victory over the Canaanite army. All that remained for him to have the honor of winning was to capture Sisera. But Deborah had prophesied that the honor for the victory would elude him and be taken by a woman. Jael saw him coming by and went out to meet him saying, "Come, and I will show you the man whom you are seeking." He probably expected to find Sisera huddled in a corner under guard and an easy target. Instead he saw him lying dead with a peg through his head (v. 22).

All at once Barak's glory has gone and been taken by Jael. Deborah had made a double prophecy that had been perfectly fulfilled. Sisera had been delivered into Barak's hands (v. 7), but in the end the Lord delivered him into the hands of a woman (v. 9). *She* now had the honor, but Barak was still the hero. Yes, he showed weakness when he asked Deborah to go with him, but he acted in faith, and thereby won the victory.

The victory over Sisera broke the power of King Jabin and strengthened the Israelites. Soon they had gained the ascendancy in Galilee. They defeated and destroyed King Jabin and his capital, Hazor (vv. 23-24). The point of this story is not to raise moral problems for discussion (like the instance here of Jael's murdering a man) but to report that God was saving His people by subduing the Canaanites.

The Song of Deborah (5:1-31)

To celebrate the victory over the Canaanite coalition and the killing of Sisera, Deborah and Barak sang a hymn. It is called the "Song of Deborah" and is widely recognized as a magnificent example of Hebrew poetry. Like the Song of Moses in Exodus 15, it expresses thanks to God as the true Victor over the horses and chariots of the enemy. In this study we will consider only its major themes, leaving a number of technical questions for deeper investigation.

An Invitation to Praise (5:1-5)

The first verse is an introduction. The song then begins with an invitation to bless (praise) the Lord. The reason to praise is that both the Israelite leaders, and the people have dedicated themselves to do God's will. These would include Deborah, Barak, and the Israelite volunteers who joined the army (v. 2). Deborah wants the kings of the Canaanites to know that the true Victor was the "LORD, the God of Israel." He covenanted to defeat their gods and give the land to His people (vv. 3 and 5).

Deborah praised God for His intervention at Mount Sinai and His provision in the wilderness through Seir and Edom to the Promised Land (vv. 4-5). Baal, the storm god of the Canaanites, had been defeated and humiliated by the storm that God sent in the Valley of Kishon. "The clouds dropped water; the mountains quaked before the LORD."

Leaders to Face the Crisis (5:6-8)

Along with the ascendancy of Yahweh to assist Israel, Deborah now describes her own rise to leadership in this time of oppression and weakness. In the days of Shamgar and Jael, commerce was halted, travel was limited, and village life was curtailed. Then God sent Deborah the prophetess to give them guidance as a "mother in Israel." Verse 8 is difficult but best understood when translated "God chose new leaders," probably referring to Deborah and Barak. Although the Israelites had no weapons, God would use the new leaders He chose in spite of their weakness.

Everyone Speaks of Yahweh's Triumph (5:9-11)

In this section the rulers of Israel are marching out to battle led by Deborah and Barak who are following the Lord. God's triumphs will be their triumphs, so they are to bless God in thanksgiving. But the rich Canaanite rulers who had smugly carried on their trade with white donkeys and fancy clothes for so long while the Israelites languished were now the losers. Deborah scornfully asks them to join the Israelites in singing. Even the people at the wells, where local news and gossip was usually shared, would recount the righteous acts of the Lord in the Israelite victory.

The Response of the Tribes to the Call to Battle (5:12-18)

Winning the battle at the Kishon was not enough, however. Now they had to take their God-given responsibilities to lead the nation. Verse 13 appears to be obscure in our version but it indicates that God's people responded to the call to arms. She praised the tribes who followed Barak into battle (Ephraim, Benjamin, and Machir, which was the half of Manasseh on the west bank, v. 14). Issachar was marked out for special praise as that tribe stayed at Barak's heels, as well as Zebulun, who put their lives in jeopardy, and Naphtali who fought in the high places, the hottest part of the battle. These are examples to believers who face the enemy hosts in high places, for whom God has provided protective "armor" (Eph. 6:11).

It was the Lord's battle, not Barak's.

But others did not come. Reuben had great resolves of heart but remained at home by the sheepfolds, Gilead stayed beyond the Jordan, Dan remained on his ships, and Asher stayed home by the seashore (vv. 15b-17).

The Battle Described and Concluded (5:19-31)

Deborah's song of praise now addresses the most critical point of the battle, which occurred at Taanach near Megiddo. This is where the heavy and unexpected rains descended, turning the valley into a bog. It immobilized the chariots; and then the River Kishon flooded and swept them away. The men of Meroz had decided not to come and the angel of the Lord commanded a curse on them (v. 23). In contrast to the curse on Meroz is the blessing on Jael, who risked her life when she had opportunity to kill Sisera (cf. 4:19-21). The song then describes Sisera's mother waiting in vain for his return while she imagines the spoil he has collected. It ends with a prayer that the enemies of the Lord may perish and those who love Him be like the sun shining in all its glory and strength (v. 31). Sisera's defeat resulted in forty years of peace for Israel.

Lessons of Leadership from Deborah

1. She understood the disintegration of her society. In it she saw a need and responded to the call of God.
2. She obtained help—she sent for Barak. She knew her own limitations and strengths. She was a motivator and knew Barak's strengths. He had already distinguished himself as a soldier and it was to him that she appealed for military leadership.
3. She motivated him in three ways. First, she *confronted him* with God's command saying, "Has not the Lord God of Israel commanded?" (4:6). Second, she *strengthened him* with God's promise, "I will deliver him [Sisera] into your hand" (4:7). Third, she *encouraged him* with her presence saying, "I will surely go with you" (4:9).

LESSON 4 EXAM

Use the answer sheet that has been provided to complete your exam.

1. **The next oppression, described in Judges 4, was by**
   A. a coalition of foreign kings.
   B. a coalition of Canaanite kings.
   C. a king from the south.
   D. a king from east of the Jordan.

2. **____________ was the commander of the coalition army.**
   A. Jabin
   B. Barak
   C. Jael
   D. Sisera

3. **As a prophetess, Deborah**
   A. gave the people God's answer to the oppression of Jabin.
   B. foretold the distant future of the nation.
   C. instructed the people to move back to Egypt.
   D. had large meetings to increase her fame.

4. **Prophets were people who primarily**
   A. were the leaders of the nation.
   B. could see into the future.
   C. received a revelation from God and communicated it to people.
   D. were the historians of the nation.

5. **The Lord told Deborah to gather 10,000 men from ____________ at Mt. Tabor.**
   A. Judah and Simeon
   B. Dan and Issachar
   C. Zebulun and Naphtali
   D. Ephraim and Manasseh

6. **Barak agreed to lead the Israelite army if**
   A. Deborah would go with him.
   B. Deborah would gather the troops.
   C. his wife would allow it.
   D. the Israelites would pay him.

7. **Sisera and his army was defeated by**
   A. Barak.
   B. the Lord.
   C. Deborah.
   D. Jabin.

8. **When Sisera saw his army being defeated he**
   A. rallied his soldiers and fought harder.
   B. led his army in retreat.
   C. initiated a new strategy.
   D. ran away from the battle.

9. **Heber's wife Jael welcomed Sisera into her tent and then**
   A. killed him.
   B. protected him.
   C. sent him out the back way.
   D. gave him a message for the king.

10. **Chapter 5 of Judges is**
   A. a blow-by-blow account of the battle.
   B. a hymn of confession and repentance.
   C. a hymn of thanks to God for victory.
   D. a list of plans for the future.

What Do You Say?

What are some lessons of leadership from the example of Deborah? How can you apply them to your situation?

LESSON 5

Gideon, Prepared for Leadership

Judges 6:1-24

After the great victory of Deborah and Barak over Jabin, the king of the Canaanites, the land had peace for forty years (1237 – 1198 BC). Then once again the nation of Israel "did what was evil in the sight of the LORD," and the Lord delivered them into the hand of Midian for seven years. It was then that God raised up a man named Gideon to lead them to victory and to rule as a judge in Israel. The story of Gideon is an encouraging example of how God worked in the life of a frightened farmer and used him mightily so that his name is listed among the heroes of faith in Hebrews 11. We meet Gideon at a point where many of us are in our Christian experience, living in the spiritual shadows and making almost no impact on the world around us for God's glory. When God looks at us He sees us not for what we are now, but for what we can become when we allow Him to take over in our lives. He takes our weakness and transforms it into abilities that can be used for His glory.

The Oppression of the Midianites (6:1-6)

The Midianites were the descendants of Midian, the son of Abraham by his second wife, Keturah (Gen. 25:2). His descendants had multiplied to become a strong nation of bedouins; they controlled the camel caravan trade routes across the desert. Midianites were those who sold Joseph into slavery (Genesis 37). Moses married the daughter of Jethro, a Midianite priest. In the time of the judges they took advantage of the weakness of Israel. They joined with the Amalekites in the south and the Arabians of the east to conduct annual raids against Israel.

A Cavalry of Camels

The Midianites used camels to great advantage in battle. Camels could carry large loads for great distances without food or water. The Israelites had tried to repulse Midian, but the power of Midian "overpowered Israel" (v. 2). The Midianite soldiers seemed as numerous as a swarm of locusts and their camels, likewise, seemed to be without number (v. 5). The Midianite raids so intimidated the Israelites that instead of resisting them, they left their farms to hide in the mountains and in caves with as much produce as possible.

In the time of the judges, Midianites invaded Israel every year at harvest time in order to steal all the harvested grain and the livestock and take it all back to their own country (vv. 4-5). Their target areas were the Valley of Jezreel from Bethshan to Mount Carmel and south along the coast as far as Gaza. These were, and still are, the best farming areas of Israel. After seven years of this outrageous robbery, the Israelites were desperately poor and finally cried out to the Lord (v. 6). It took them that long to discern that God was "speaking" to them. Israel's dilemma in those times illustrates that of many Christians today who have been brought low by the invasion of the enemy armies of secular humanism, self-centeredness, and materialism. And like Israel then, we fail to recognize God's chastising.

A Prophet Explains Their Trial (6:7-10)

Every other time the Israelites cried to God He had sent them a judge. This time, however, He sent a prophet, because their greatest need was spiritual. The prophet had a message from God for them. Like other prophets in Old Testament times he probably moved from one community to another repeating the message from God. He began with the typical prophetic introduction, "Thus says the LORD ..." They had cried for help, and this was God's answer. The Israelites had not confessed their sin and it would be logical to suppose that God would send His prophet to pronounce judgment on them. But notice what God does say through His unnamed servant.

He reminded them of God's faithfulness and His grace to them when He rescued them from their slavery in Egypt. In six sharp statements the prophet reminded how it was God who had done everything to bring them from hopeless slavery to victorious freedom in their own land. In effect God said:

- I brought you up from Egypt.
- I brought you out of the house of bondage.

- I delivered you out of the hand of the Egyptians.
- I delivered you out of the hand of all who oppressed you on the way.
- I drove out your enemies in the land of Canaan.
- I gave you their land as your possession.

With Yahweh on their side, the Israelites had no reason to fear Canaanite gods. The unnamed prophet closed his message with God's explanation for their present distressing situation: "you have not obeyed My voice" (v. 10). He wanted them to understand that He had heard *their* voice, but they had not listened to *His*. Though He had given them innumerable mercies along the way, they only thought of themselves and how to get out of the mess they were in. God wanted them to understand their own disobedience first. So He allowed them to be invaded by the Midianites for seven straight years.

God still uses unnamed servants to impact our lives. The prophet's words were only the first step in their restoration. Then they heard the report that the Midianites were coming for the eighth time, and they still had no promise of a deliverer.

The Call of Gideon (6:11-16)

The story moves on from the message of the prophet to the call and the preparation of a deliverer from the tribe of Manasseh named Gideon. His father, Joash, was influential as a cult leader in the village of Ophrah near the city of Megiddo. Gideon was the youngest of his sons in a small clan and was the only survivor, because the Midianites had killed his brothers (8:18-19). The Israelite nation was at an all-time low point and Gideon's family had very little status.

Gideon the Farmer (6:11)

We are introduced to Gideon as a village farmer threshing wheat. Normally wheat was threshed near the field where it was grown by using a pair of oxen dragging a large flat stone in circles over the grain on a hardened area called a threshing floor. The stone crushed the wheat, separating the kernels from the husks. However, because of the threat of the Midianites, Gideon was not doing it that way. Instead of using oxen to thresh the wheat on a threshing floor, he brought the bundles of wheat home and put it in a winepress under a tree. He was trying to thresh it by beating it with a stick—a most inefficient process. Then he would hide the threshed wheat hoping that the Midianites would not find it. Evidently the Midianites had not yet crossed the Jordan into Israel that year (vv. 11, 33). The description of Gideon indicates a struggling farmer, the son of a village cult leader, and the only remaining member of his family. He was fearful of the enemy and deeply humiliated. But God had His eye on him.

A Visit from the Angel (6:12)

Unlike most of the Israelites, Gideon was still a worshipper of the one true God (Yahweh). He had not bowed down to the Canaanite god Baal, even though his father was a priest of Baal. Then one day, while he was threshing the bundles of wheat by the winepress, an unknown "person" came near and sat under the tree. Gideon didn't know how long he had been there.

He had no idea that the unknown man was an angel; in fact he was more than an angel. He was the Angel of the Lord. He was no less a figure than the second Person of the Trinity. He was God. The Angel suddenly now made himself known to Gideon. He said, "The Lord is with you, O mighty man of valor." It was a title of honor, but there seemed little about Gideon to merit it. Most commentators view the Angel's greeting as a prophetic statement about what Gideon was to become.

Mighty men of valor were brave soldiers willing to face a superior enemy (Josh. 10:7). Gideon would surely become a man like that. It seems that God knew his heart. But at this low point he was doggedly doing what had to be done to meet the daily needs of his family (v. 12). He did not look like a mighty man of valor and nor did he yet feel like the Lord was with him.

Gideon's Questions (6:13-14)

Gideon was discouraged, and he answered the Angel with a series of rhetorical questions. He saw no evidence that the Lord was with him. He is like so many of God's people today who know what God has done in the past, but do not believe that God will act like that in the present. He couldn't believe that the Lord was with him, in the midst of hiding there trying to thresh a little wheat.

To the words of the Angel, "The LORD is with you" (singular), Gideon replied that he saw no evidence of God's presence with "us" (plural). In his doubt he said, "if the LORD is with us, why then has all this happened to us?" And he went on to complain that there were no miracles happening as had happened to their fathers. He thought God had turned His back on the Israelites, but the truth was that the Israelites had turned their backs on God. Gideon was doing just what we are so quick to do. When bad things happen, we tend to blame anything but ourselves. We are very slow to look in the mirror.

But notice that the Angel did not rebuke Gideon. He seemed to pay little attention to his questions and doubts. Instead He turned to look at him and commanded him, "Go in this might of yours." The phrase does not refer to Gideon's natural strength, but to the strength that God would give him as he obeyed. Then after the Angel commanded him to save Israel He reminded Gideon that he had all the authority he needed to go. He said, "Do not I send you?"

There are several parallels between Gideon's commission and Christ's Great Commission of the disciples (Matt. 28:18-20). Hudson Taylor, the founder of the China Inland Mission, said, "All of God's great men have been weak men who did great things for God because they knew that God had sent them and they reckoned on God being with them."

Gideon's Objection (6:15)

When God told Gideon to "go," Gideon replied that he was too small for the job and that he did not have any qualifications. Gideon was actually overstating his inability. We have already mentioned that his family had some influence and standing in the community. But like Moses in Exodus 3, he felt completely inadequate. Compare Exodus 3:10-12 with Judges 6:14-16 and you will find several close similarities between the excuses of the two men and the answers that God gave to them. It may be that the parallels are intentional, but we cannot know for certain. It is actually good to understand that we are not capable or competent for the job God may be calling us to do. Our competency comes from God. So away with self-confidence, and let us remember that we are meant to depend on God (2 Cor. 3:5).

With Yahweh on their side, the Israelites had no reason to fear Canaanite gods.

God's Assurance of His Presence and Victory (6:16)

God gave Gideon two words of encouragement. The first was the guarantee of God's presence that would transform Gideon from a wimp into a warrior. Notice that the presence of the Lord has been the centerpiece of each of the Lord's three statements to Gideon (vv. 12, 14, 16): I am with you, I have sent you, and I am with you. The second word of encouragement was the guarantee of an easy victory. It would be so easy that the Midianites would be defeated as if his whole army was fighting just one man.

The Authenticating Sign (6:17-21)

Gideon then asked his Visitor for two things: for a sign that would confirm to him what He had said, and that He not leave until he had brought an offering (vv. 17-18). By this time Gideon had understood that the Visitor was no ordinary man or angel. Only God could do what this Person was promising to do. So he responded by asking the Angel of the Lord to confirm the commission by giving him a special sign. He wanted to prepare and bring a meal as an offering of worship and a sign that the Angel would accept the offering. Like most offerings, this was to be an offering of food. The size of it indicates it was given to God. The Angel agreed to wait (v. 18). Gideon then prepared an entire kid, bread made from an ephah of flour (about 35 pounds), and some broth.

Gideon rightly became conscious of his unworthiness to be in God's presence.

When the meal was all prepared, Gideon brought it all to the Angel of the Lord, who was still sitting under the tree. The Angel instructed Gideon to place the bread and the meat on a certain rock, just as he would put an offering on the altar. Then He told Gideon to take the broth and pour it over the meat and bread on the rock altar. The Angel then reached out with His staff and touched the offering with the end of it. Immediately fire appeared from the rock and burned up the offering. When Gideon looked up, the Angel was gone, but three things were clear to him (v. 21). First, the miraculous fire gave him the assurance that he had been speaking with God. Second, he knew that he had found favor with God when God accepted the sacrifice. Third, he realized that he had been in the presence of God.

Confession and Worship (6:22-24)

Having now realized that he had been in God's presence, Gideon rightly became conscious of his unworthiness to be there. He cried out in fear, "Alas, O Lord GOD! For now I have seen the angel of the LORD face to face." It appears he thought that anyone who saw God would die (Ex. 33:20; cf. Gen. 16:13; 32:30; Ex. 20:19; 1 Tim. 6:16), for although the

Lord was no longer visible, He answered Gideon directly saying, "Peace be to you. Do not fear; you shall not die" (v. 23). So the first thing that Gideon did was humble himself in God's presence. The second thing that Gideon did was to worship God. He immediately built an altar and called it Jehovah Shalom, meaning *the Lord is Peace*, because the Lord had said "Peace be to you" (v. 23). Then the altar remained there as a memorial of Gideon's encounter with the Lord and the promise of peace. God gave Gideon personal peace with Himself, and He also promised Israel peace and deliverance from their enemies.

LESSON 5 EXAM

Use the answer sheet that has been provided to complete your exam.

1. **When Israel once again turned away from God after the victory of Deborah and Barak, He sent __________ to oppress them.**
   A. the Philistines
   B. the Jebusites
   C. Midian
   D. King Jabin

2. **Which man did God use to rescue them?**
   A. Gideon
   B. Jephthath
   C. Samuel
   D. Abimelech

3. **The Midianites made annual raids into Israel at**
   A. the beginning of the year.
   B. harvest time.
   C. the end of the year.
   D. sheep-shearing time.

4. **God sent a message to the Israelites through a prophet**
   A. to remind them of His faithfulness and grace.
   B. to pronounce judgment because of their sins.
   C. to announce the name of the new deliverer.
   D. to prepare them for a change of government.

5. **Because of the threat of the Midianites, Gideon**
   A. did not plant crops.
   B. threshed his wheat in a wine press.
   C. went into hiding.
   D. gathered an army to confront them.

6. **Gideon was a worshipper of**
   A. Baal.
   B. Molech.
   C. Ashteroth.
   D. Yahweh.

7. **The person who appeared to Gideon was**
   A. a prophet.
   B. a neighbor.
   C. the village leader.
   D. the Angel of the Lord.

8. Like Gideon, our capacity for a task must come from

A. God.
B. our innate gifts.
C. our training.
D. our heritage.

9. Gideon asked his visitor for a sign that would

A. show him what to do next.
B. confirm what He had said.
C. indicate who should go with him.
D. convince his father to agree.

10. Gideon built an altar and called it

A. "the Lord is our Helper."
B. "the Lord is our Provider."
C. "the Lord is Peace."
D. "the Lord is mighty."

What Do You Say?

Has your spiritual life been compromised by the "invasion" of the philosophies of this world? What have you done/will you do about it?

LESSON 6

Gideon, Tested for Battle

Judges 6:25-40

The Commandment to Destroy the Pagan Altar (6:25)

That same night the Lord spoke to Gideon, perhaps in a dream or vision, and told him to offer another sacrifice. This time it would stir up a great deal of opposition from the local Baal worshippers. Evidently his father Joash had built an altar to Baal on his own property, and the village people used this shrine in their worship of Baal. It was the centerpiece of the village shrine that included an idol of Baal and an Asherah pole for his female consort. Idols of Baal and Asherah poles were common in Canaanite fertility cults. There still exists an ancient altar to Baal twenty-six feet square at Megiddo only a few miles from Ophrah.

It should be no surprise that Joash had a pagan shrine on his property. Like many people today he had succumbed to the pervasive influence of the world. Baal worship then, like the idols of our world today, promised to meet his hopes and desires for pleasure, possessions, and power, but never really delivered. As long as that pagan altar was in Gideon's backyard he could not lead the people to victory in the Name of Yahweh the true God. Victory for God must begin at home. We cannot please God or serve Him acceptably while we give priority to the idols of the world.

The Ultimate Indignity to Baal (6:26)

After tearing down the altar and its idols, God told Gideon to build a new altar on "the stronghold here" or rock (perhaps on the village wall) in the name of Yahweh. Then he was to slaughter his father's seven-year-old prize bull and offer it as an offering to the Lord on the altar he had built. The fuel for the fire on the altar in this public place would be his father's wooden idols connected with Baal. Doing that publicly would demonstrate to the whole community that he had committed himself 100 percent to God and 100 percent in opposition to Baal. In this way God tested his obedience in a smaller job before sending him to lead an army of 30,000.

There has been much discussion by Bible commentators over whether the text in verse 25 is talking about two bulls or one. It is best to take it that the words "young bull" refer to a "prime bull," a bull of superior quality which is seven years old, then to take the words translated "second bull" in the NKJV of verse 26 to mean an exalted bull, or one of high rank. Thus the bull belonging to Gideon's father is his prize seven-year-old bull. Gideon was to use the bull to pull down the pagan altar, to build another altar in the Name of Yahweh, and then to take the same bull and sacrifice it to the living God.

The whole incident was the ultimate indignity to the false god of Baal, and it was an insult to all the villagers who were Baal worshippers. Gideon knew that doing this meant there was going to be trouble.

There are some great lessons here for us:

- God's altar cannot be built until Baal's altar is destroyed. Too many of God's people are practicing modern-day idolatry with worldly idols such as popularity, money, position, and pleasure. Then they wonder why the worship of God seems so dull and formal and why their personal spiritual lives lack power and vitality. The Lord's altar and Baal's altar cannot both exist alongside one another.
- You must win victories at home before God will trust you with victories on a larger scale.

Gideon's Obedience (6:27)

In obedience to God, Gideon took ten of his trusted servants to help him. He worked at night because he knew that his father would have tried to stop him. Some have thought that asking the ten men to help him and working at night were signs of Gideon's lack of faith. More than likely, the reason for doing it that way was because of the size of the job God had asked him to do.

Was Gideon afraid? Certainly he was. But fear would not stop him being obedient. It says, "did as the LORD had told him" (v. 27). It is a scary thing to be obedient when you are sure that there will be consequences. Paul overcame his fear and wrote to the Corinthians, "I was with you in weakness and in fear and much trembling" (1 Cor. 2:3-4). To confess Christ today in a land that promotes another religion is to overcome fear and weakness. When you sense your own weakness while you are doing God's will, it is then that you are really strong. Perhaps Gideon was not being a great hero when he got others to help and by working at night, but he was being obedient. It was obedience that was essential; heroism was optional.

Joash Challenges Baal (6:28-32)

Gideon completed the destruction of the idols and the building of the altar by dawn. When the men of the city saw the prize bull being burned as an offering to Yahweh, they were angry and immediately wanted to know who did it. One of Gideon's servants who had participated in the act must have revealed that the culprit was "Gideon the son of Joash." The townspeople went and told Joash that Gideon should be put to death. How far the Israelites had fallen from the time of Moses, when the standard was that Israelites who practiced idolatry were to be stoned to death (Deut. 13:6-10)! Now the Israelites were demanding that the person who destroyed the idol in the name of God was to be stoned (v. 30).

We cannot please God while we give priority to the idols of the world.

Joash refused to put Gideon to death. He argued that if Baal was a god he could defend himself. He went on to say, "Will you contend [plead] for Baal?" He meant, does Baal need our help to deal with my son? If Baal doesn't need us, it would be an insult to him if we interfere. An insult would be punishable by death. If he is really a god, let him plead for himself and punish Gideon as he sees fit. It is his altar that has been torn down. This argument won the day. Nothing happened to Gideon, but something happened to the people. They saw the reality of Gideon's commitment and they gave him a new name, Jerubbaal, which means "Let Baal contend." The name soon came to mean "Baal-fighter."

Gideon's reputation had now risen from a man out of step with his generation to a man that people looked to for direction. It all happened because he was willing to obey God and pull down the altar of Baal. God suddenly brought him into public leadership and usefulness because he was willing to put his life on the line when God said, "Act!"

Clothed with the Holy Spirit (6:33-35)

The local crisis over Gideon's action in Ophrah was soon set aside because of the invasion of the Midianite/Amalekite coalition. They swarmed across the Jordan into the Valley of Jezreel and made their camp there. Wheat harvest was ready at the time of Pentecost (May-June). For seven years they had invaded this rich farmland and carried off their grain harvest and their domestic animals without a fight. But it would be different this year. Why? Because the Spirit of the Lord had come upon Gideon (v. 34).

Literally, verse 34 says, "The Spirit of the Lord clothed Himself around Gideon," as it were, like armor, so that he was now under the power and control of the Holy Spirit of God. As Christian believers, we are not *clothed* with the Spirit of God but indwelled by Him permanently. In Old Testament times, however, the Holy Spirit came *on* His chosen instruments. The same wording is used in 2 Chronicles 24:20 when the Spirit of God "clothed" Zechariah the priest so that he boldly charged the people with apostasy (forsaking God), and again, when the Spirit clothed a soldier named Amasai who committed himself to David (1 Chron. 12:18).

Should Christians use Gideon's example as a model for obtaining guidance?

The Spirit clothed Gideon to defeat the Midianites. He acted right away and blew the trumpet—a trumpet of alarm, so that people would gather as an army to face the enemy. The first to gather were the Abiezrites, his own relatives. Then he sent some of the Abiezrites as messengers to invite the tribes of Manasseh, Asher, Zebulun, and Naphtali to join them. These were all northern tribes in that area (v. 34). The tribe of Ephraim was not invited, perhaps because they were the largest and most arrogant of the tribes and Gideon was from Manasseh, a smaller tribe (cf. 8:1-3). God's timing was perfect, for just as the enemy approached, and the news of Gideon's courage spread, the trumpet called them to action.

Notice three things about Gideon that apply to us if we are to be effective servants of the Lord Jesus Christ:

- He had a personal encounter with the Angel of the Lord—for us, the Lord Jesus Christ.
- He had disciplined himself to obey God publicly, even at high risk.
- He was empowered by the Holy Spirit.

The Sign of the Fleece (6:36-40)

Gideon then proceeded to ask and receive a sign from God. He told God that he would put a lamb's wool fleece on the threshing floor at night. If the fleece was wet in the morning, but the ground was dry, it would signify that God would deliver Israel by using him as its leader. God honored his request the next morning. Gideon was still not convinced and thus asked God to do it the other way around the following morning. Once again God honored his request and the fleece was dry, while the ground was wet.

Gideon's dealing with God over the fleece has become the basis for some believers today when wanting God's direction or blessing. God was gracious to honor Gideon's request, but should Christians use his example as a model for obtaining guidance? Consider the following:

- Gideon already knew what God wanted him to do. He admitted it twice in his prayer, "You will save Israel by my hand, as you have said" (vv. 36-37). God had already started to save Israel when he blew the trumpet to gather the soldiers. Over 30,000 of them had responded. But still Gideon was not really sure that God would fulfill His word.
- Gideon's fleece was evidence of his doubt, not his faith. God had given him a sign (v. 21), but he wanted another. Gideon had been chosen by God, informed of his task, and empowered by the Spirit for this task. His army had gathered and he had experienced Yahweh's protection when he tore down the pagan altar. Even with all that, Gideon held back from obeying. He prayed to God, but notice that he does not pray in the name of Yahweh (God's personal name) who made covenant with Israel, but uses the generic name for God the Creator—Elohim. Gideon admits that what he did was a "test" of Yahweh (v. 39), just as Israel had "tested" the Lord at Rephidim (Ex. 17:2-7).
- Telling God what to do was presumptuous. Gideon was dictating to God. He was putting God in a box. However, we must not be too critical of Gideon as he had already committed himself to God, but at this point he was not acting in faith.
- Gideon's problem would never be solved by fleece. Whether the fleece was dry or wet, it did not give him certainty. Even after wringing a bowl full of water from the wet fleece he asked for

another test. He could never be certain that some fluke in the climate had not caused it. For Gideon the divinely chosen sign had already been given to him. The offering had been accepted, the plan of God clearly revealed, and 32,000 men had responded to the call. He needed no further sign. But God knew his frailty and remembered that he was dust (Ps. 103:14). How gracious God was with him in spite of his faults!

Knowing God's Will

The Bible says, "Do not be foolish, but understand what the will of the Lord is" (Eph. 5:17). Some people have tested God by telling Him something like this: "Lord, I have plan 'A' and plan 'B.' If you want me to follow plan 'A' then have 'so and so' phone me by 6 p.m. on Tuesday. If the call does not come by then I will follow plan 'B.'" How much better to wait on the Lord in prayer that He will, in His own time and way, assure you of His guidance in a matter! Consider some great promises from God about His way of guidance.

- "I will instruct you and teach you in the way you should go; I will counsel you with my eye upon you." Psalm 32:8
- "The steps of a man are established by the Lord,when he delights in his way; though he fall, he shall not be cast headlong, for the Lord upholds his hand." Psalm 37:23-24
- "That this is God, our God forever and ever. He will guide us forever." Psalm 48:14

Principles of Guidance

- The Guide is more important than the guidance. Gideon had had a personal encounter with the divine Guide, the Second Person of the Trinity. From this encounter he knew what he should do. God's will has more to do with our relationship with the Guide than knowing a set of mechanical rules.
- Guidance is based on the precepts of the Word of God, that is, by obeying what you already know in the Word. God is concerned first about what you *are.* When you are what He wants you to be, you will have little difficulty with the issue of guidance.

- When we are in conscious fellowship with God and delighting in Him, He gives us a desire for what pleases Him. The desire of our heart will be to bring Him glory (Ps. 37:3-4).
- Guidance comes also from the counsel of godly and experienced believers.

LESSON 6 EXAM

Use the answer sheet that has been provided to complete your exam.

1. **Gideon's experience shows us that victory for God**
   A. must have the cooperation of others.
   B. should begin at home.
   C. will take time.
   D. will make us popular.

2. **God tested Gideon's obedience in a smaller job by telling him to**
   A. build an altar and offer a sacrifice to the Lord.
   B. gather 30,000 men to fight the Midianites.
   C. confront his family about their Baal worship.
   D. finish threshing the wheat to feed his family.

3. **We cannot worship and enjoy God if we**
   A. don't follow the proper liturgy.
   B. are giving priority to worldly idols.
   C. associate with unbelievers.
   D. don't go to church regularly.

4. **When Gideon tore down the shrine to Baal and built an altar to God, he**
   A. worked alone at night.
   B. worked alone all day.
   C. worked at night with 10 other men.
   D. worked for a week with 10 other men.

5. **Gideon was obedient even though he was**
   A. tired.
   B. alone.
   C. afraid.
   D. confused.

6. **Gideon was able to defeat the Midianites because**
   A. he was well-organized.
   B. the Spirit of the Lord came upon him.
   C. he was a good leader.
   D. he had a large army.

7. **The account of Gideon and "his fleece" was evidence of his**
   A. doubt.
   B. faith.
   C. courage.
   D. commitment.

8. **__________ explains God's gracious response to Gideon's request concerning the fleece.**
   A. Psalm 103:14
   B. Psalm 77:17
   C. Isaiah 13:9
   D. Deuteronomy 32:19

9. **God's will has more to do with**
   A. knowing a set of mechanical rules.
   B. considering all possible complications.
   C. having a close relationship with Him.
   D. considering a variety of options.

10. **Guidance is *based* on**
    A. thoughtful consideration of the issues.
    B. knowing and obeying the precepts of the Word of God.
    C. consulting with others in the situation.
    D. understanding what will be best for our life.

What Do You Say?

As you consider your service for Christ, how has He prepared you for the task He has given you?

LESSON 7

Gideon, Faithful in Battle

Judges 7:1–8:35

Time after time, when the Israelites had turned away from God, He disciplined them by allowing their enemies to harass them in their land. When the crisis became intolerable, they cried to the Lord and He sent a judge to deliver them. Following the initial conquering of the land under Joshua, God had provided, up until this point in their history, four such judges.

- He gave them Othniel to deliver them from the Mesopotamians.
- He gave them Ehud to deliver them from the Moabites.
- He gave them Shamgar to deliver them from the Philistines.
- He gave them Deborah and Barak to deliver them from Canaanites in the north.

Now, in this cycle, He was preparing Gideon to deliver them from the Midianites. In this period, the Midianites were God's disciplinary rod to bring the Israelites back to Himself. Over the course of seven years they invaded the land and stole the harvest. Eventually the Israelites cried to the Lord (6:7). He answered by preparing Gideon to be their judge (6:11). Gideon had set up his army on the slopes of Mount Gilboa, called Mount Gilead in this chapter. At its base was a spring called Harod from which they could see the Midianites encamped in the Valley of Jezreel. The stage for a battle was set. The Midianites outnumbered Israelites greatly—135,000 to Israel's 32,000. They were "like locusts in abundance" with a large cavalry of camels (cf. v. 12).

God Prepares Gideon and His Army for Victory (7:1-15)

Gideon's encounter with the Angel of the Lord by the winepress and his obedience in replacing Baal's altar with an altar to Yahweh had prepared him for leadership. But Gideon now needed to learn to have greater dependence on God. Perhaps he took too literally God's command to "go in this might of yours" (6:14). God loves to do great things through insignificant people who put their confidence in *Him*.

Too Many (7:1-3)

The word of God came to Gideon: "The people with you are too many for Me." In other words, "If all 32,000 of them go with you, they may claim the credit for winning the battle." Dependence on God is one of the great principles of spiritual warfare. So God gave Gideon two tests to determine who and how many should go into the battle. The first test was to weed out those who were afraid. He told Gideon to announce that any who were afraid were free to go home in case they discouraged the others with their fears (cf. Deut. 20:8). We don't know whether Gideon was surprised or not, but 22,000 men withdrew, leaving only 10,000 in the camp. That eliminated the two-thirds of them who saw the enemy as bigger than God (v. 3).

Still Too Many! (7:4-8)

God looked at the 10,000 who remained and said to Gideon, "The people are still too many." So He gave Gideon a second test that was not at first obvious. He said, "Take them down to the water," that is, to the stream flowing from the spring. The Lord continued, "I will test them for you there." None of the participants knew what the test was about. The soldiers would all have opportunity to drink from the stream. As they drank, most of them got down on all fours and put their mouths in the water and drank their fill. They forgot all about the enemy and concentrated on drinking. But 300 of those 10,000 were aware of the enemy presence and the possible threat of an attack. They never took their eyes off the enemy, even for a drink of water. So when they came to the stream they simply dipped their hands into the water and lapped it from their hands like a dog.

Then God said to Gideon, "With the 300 men who lapped I will save you and give the Midianites into your hand." Observe:

- When Gideon first called for an army, only 32,000 of those called were even *ready* to show up.
- Of those 32,000, only 10,000 who saw the size of the enemy were *courageous* enough to stay and fight.
- Of those 10,000, only 300 were *committed* enough to deny themselves and watch out for the enemy. The others may have been fearless, but they were careless. But 300 were ready, courageous, and committed to get the job done.

God is not looking for high-profile Christians, but for faithful Christians who depend on Him, who trust Him completely and obey Him willingly. Gideon's men were now outnumbered 443 to 1; but they were not thinking of the human odds—they were resting on divine power. Then before the 9,700 left, Gideon collected all the *shofar* horns of the commanders.

The Barley Bun and the Toppled Tent (7:9-15)

God knew that Gideon still needed to learn to have greater confidence in Him, however. So in the middle of the night God said to him, "Arise, go down against the camp, for I have given it into your hand. But if you are afraid to go down, go down to the camp with Purah your servant." Note that Gideon *was* still afraid (v. 10), and now God was exposing his fear. The author repeats that the Midianites and their cavalry of camels were innumerable (v. 12). Gideon woke Purah and they went to the edge of the enemy camp. They overheard two Midianites talking inside their tent. One was telling the other that he had dreamed about a small barley loaf that tumbled into their camp. The loaf struck a tent that completely collapsed on impact. Obviously, God had sent this dream.

God loves to do great things through insignificant people who put their confidence in Him.

His friend in the tent immediately interpreted the dream. He explained that the barley loaf referred to Israel (which was using barley to make bread because the Midianites were stealing all the wheat). And the tent referred to the Midianites, who were nomadic and lived in tents. Gideon would attack the Midianite camp and knock it down. He concluded, "This is no other than the sword of Gideon ... God has given into his hand Midian and all the camp" (v. 14). The barley loaf "tumbled" into the camp. The word means "overthrow," so Gideon's men would "overthrow" the Midianites.

When Gideon and Purah heard this, their hearts must have skipped a beat. Only the Sovereign God could cause them to arrive undetected at the exact moment, allow them to overhear that conversation about the dream, and then hear them say that Gideon was "the sword of the LORD" who would defeat them.

Gideon at last believed that God would give him the victory. He saw that it was God who would win the battle, and he and his men were no more than God's instruments. God had already spread the fear of the Israelites among the Midianites. There is no other way to interpret verses 13 and 14. Otherwise, why would they be afraid of 300 men whose captain had no military experience? Now there was no reason for Gideon to doubt, so Gideon fell on his face in grateful worship (v. 15). Gideon was stripped down to the place where he realized he could not depend on himself. Now he could be fully confident in God alone. He saw that he was nothing and that God was everything. One of the main lessons of this story is not the victory Gideon would win, but the change in his heart that God orchestrated.

Gideon was still afraid and now God was exposing his fear.

The Battle Plan (7:16-18)

Gideon and Purah went back to their camp. We can assume that around this time God had given Gideon the battle plan. That night, or more likely the next night, Gideon woke up his 300 men. He announced, "Arise, for the LORD has given the host of Midian into your hand" (v. 15). He armed them with the ram's horn trumpets, the kind used by army commanders to signal their companies to charge into battle. So when 300 trumpets sounded, it would give the impression to the enemy that there were 300 infantry companies of men about to charge. Gideon also armed his men with 300 empty clay jars with torches (lamps) placed inside them. These men were committed to follow instructions, whether the instructions made sense or not.

When the men were armed with their strange armor, Gideon divided them into three groups of one hundred men each. He gave them instructions to keep their eyes on him and do exactly what he did. They had four "weapons"—jars to shatter, horns to blow, torches to shine, and voices to shout. Their instructions were simply to watch Gideon and do what he did. They quietly arranged themselves on three sides of the enemy. These were the men who had passed the tests. They were ready, courageous, and committed. They did not have to be told to obey orders. "When I blow the trumpet ... then blow the trumpets also on every side of all the camp and shout, 'For the LORD and for Gideon!'" Obedience was the path to victory.

The Battle Begun (7:19-22)

The Midianites were in a deep sleep in their camp. It was the beginning of the middle watch, sometime after 10 p.m. The guard had just changed. Retiring guards were returning to their tents and the new guards were taking their posts. Suddenly the stillness of the night was shattered by 300 trumpets sounding from all sides. Then they heard the crash of 300 clay jars being broken and they saw 300 lights that appeared from specially chosen positions on hills so that the whole camp could see them. All this was followed by terrifying shouts from 300 men shouting, "A sword for the LORD and for Gideon!"

The Midianite army jumped up in the dark. They assumed that a huge army had charged their camp from three directions. They heard the shouts and were terrified. The camels stampeded and everyone panicked. In their confusion they started slaughtering one another. The 300 stood in their places as if they were the battalion commanders sounding their trumpets, waving their torches and shouting, "A sword for the LORD and for Gideon!" And the whole army of Midianites "cried out and fled." They ran away down the valley toward the cities of Beth Shittah, Abel-Meholah (west of the Jordan) and Tabbah (east of the Jordan). Gideon sent word to the nearly 32,000 who had started home from the tribes of Naphtali, Asher, and Manasseh. They returned and joined in the chase (v. 23). The Midianites were headed southeast toward Ephraim so Gideon sent word for the Ephraimites to stop them at the small rivers running into the Jordan. This they did. It must have taken several days. In the process the Ephraimites actually caught two Midianite princes, Oreb and Zeeb (v. 25).

The Complaint of the Ephraimites (8:1-3)

Ephraim was the largest of the tribes. They had not tried to stop the Midianites when they came into the land, nor had they volunteered to help Gideon. But during the Midianite retreat Gideon asked them to join the battle. They had collected many spoils and captured two of the princes. But they refused to celebrate the victory or give God thanks. They were reacting as if they were jealous that they had not been asked to join in the beginning. They resented Gideon who was from the tribe of Manasseh, and felt snubbed—a sign of immature self-centeredness.

But notice Gideon's gentle response to their complaint. He congratulated them for their part in the battle. He used the language of the vineyard. He spoke of the "gleaning of the grapes of Ephraim," that is, the spoils of battle they took were greater than the "harvest of Abiezer" (Gideon's own clan), who were the first to join the battle (6:11, 24, 34). Gideon congratulated them that their contribution was greater than that of his own clan. He may have been exaggerating, but it quieted their anger. "A soft answer turns away wrath, but a harsh word stirs up anger" (Prov. 15:1).

Gideon's Capture of the Two Kings (8:4-17)

Gideon continued with his 300 men in pursuit of the Midianites. Near the point of exhaustion they crossed the Jordan and came to two Israelite cities, Succoth and Penuel. Gideon's men were "exhausted yet pursuing" of 15,000 Midianites and two kings, Ziba and Zalmunna. Gideon legitimately requested food because the two cities had been liberated from the Midianites. But the city leaders denied Gideon's request because the kings were not yet captured (v. 6). They probably had made an alliance with the Midianites. So Gideon, as God's representative in Israel, promised judgment on them because of their contempt (vv. 7- 9). Gideon and his men surprised the Midianite kings at Karkor, killing them all except for the two kings, Ziba and Zalmunna, whom he brought back as captives. When he came to the two cities he kept his promise to punish them for holding his men in contempt (vv. 13-17).

The Midianite Kings Executed (8:18-21)

The war was over and Gideon returned home to Ophrah with his men still holding the two captured kings. These two kings had apparently murdered Gideon's brothers at some time in the past on the slopes of Mount Tabor. Gideon had not been able to avenge their deaths. Now he interrogated them and they confessed that the man they had killed closely resembled Gideon. Gideon therefore executed the two kings himself. Then he took the valuable crescent ornaments from their camels as his personal booty. This marked the end of Gideon's victory over the Midianites.

The Offer for Gideon to be King (8:22-23)

After the victory the men of Israel praised Gideon for delivering them from Midian, ignoring the fact that God had done it. Based on their idea that Gideon had delivered them, they invited him to become king over them and establish a dynasty of kings in Israel. Gideon knew that it was not God's plan for the nation to be a monarchy at that time; the Lord was to be Israel's king. The nation's government was to be a theocracy (Deut. 33:5; 1 Sam. 8:6); the judges were simply His instruments of deliverance. So Gideon answered the men of Israel, "I will not rule over you, … the LORD will rule over you" (v. 23). For Gideon, this amounted to a great moment of spiritual understanding.

We who are believers today should understand this truth, for like Israel in the time of the judges, the church is a theocracy. The Head of the church is the Lord Jesus Christ, not a human person. Church leaders are "ministers" (servants), "pastors" (shepherds), and "bishops" (overseers). They are always mentioned in the plural because there is only one Head—Christ Himself (Eph. 1:22-23; 4:15; 5:23). The tendency all through church history has been to elevate a clergy with special privileges, titles, and honor over the people. The teaching and the example of the Lord Jesus was that leaders are to be humble servants (Mark 10:42-45).

Gideon and the Ephod (8:24-28)

Midianite soldiers wore gold earrings. No doubt the Israelites collected thousands of them from the defeated Midianites. Gideon requested that the Israelite soldiers give him the earrings from the booty they had collected. The soldiers considered this a modest reward for their commander and gladly gave them to him. Their combined weight amounted to 1,700 shekels, or forty-three pounds of gold (v. 26). Gideon then took the gold and from it made an ephod (v. 27). In the Old Testament an ephod was a decorated linen apron worn only by the high priest. It became the symbol of his office. In the period of the judges the priesthood and the high priest were not exercising spiritual leadership in the nation. Some commentators suggest that Gideon wore the ephod as a priest. Nothing in the text implies this. It is more likely that the forty-three pounds of gold

The Head of the church is the Lord Jesus Christ, not a human person.

were made into a golden image of an ephod and that Gideon "put it" in his hometown of Ophrah as a thanksgiving memorial for the victory that God gave them.

Gideon had rejected the offer of being a king, but he made a terrible mistake in setting up the ephod. What he thought would be a symbol of God's victory for the Israelites became an object of worship for them—an idol. People came from all Israel to see it. Verse 27 says that then all Israel "whored after it there," that is, instead of being faithful to the true God who gave them the victory, they were unfaithful to God by worshipping the golden ephod.

What Gideon intended to be a reminder of God's faithfulness turned into an object of Israel's unfaithfulness. It was spiritual adultery in the same sense that Christians may be called adulteresses when they set their affection on the world rather than God (James 4:4). There is a powerful application here to people today who try to enhance their worship with objects and symbols that may easily replace the true glory of God.

Gideon's memorial ephod caused the Israelites to slip back into idolatry. It even became a snare to Gideon and his family. This is what images, icons, and the consecration of "holy places" have done to a large part of the professing Christian church. With their prayers and gifts to these images, God is easily relegated to second place. What Gideon should have done with his great influence was to revive the established priesthood and tabernacle worship in Shiloh that God had ordained.

Gideon's Last Forty Years (8:29-32)

The next forty years were externally peaceful, but Gideon, his household, and his people all slipped into idolatry (v. 28). It was the last period of peace mentioned in the book (cf. 3:11, 30; 5:31; 8:28). He was a judge for forty years after the victory over the Midianites. He lived in the village of Ophrah and probably only governed the nearby tribes of Manasseh, Zebulun, Asher, and Naphtali. During those years Midian was subdued and there was peace in the land. Gideon lived in luxury and had many wives and seventy sons.

Besides his wives, he had a concubine in Shechem who bore him a son named Abimelech, introduced here because of the events recorded in the next chapter. Gideon exemplified what God can do through one man who will trust Him. But afterward he failed in two areas of his life: he made the ephod that became an idol that corrupted many, and he had multiple wives against the explicit command of God (Deut. 17:17).

Apostasy Once Again (8:33-35)

When Gideon died he was buried in the tomb of his father Joash. And as soon as he died, the children of Israel "whored after the Baals and made Baal-berith their god." Baal-Berith means "Baal of the covenant." The Israelites built a temple to honor him in Shechem (9:46). Thus the people of the covenant with Yahweh turned away from Him to claim a covenant relationship with the Canaanite god Baal. This generation of Israelites forgot the Lord, who had delivered them from their enemies on every side. They deliberately left God out of their reckoning (v. 34), and even failed to show kindness or respect to the house of Jerubbaal (Gideon). Gideon's compromise at the end of his life eliminated the respect he had earned when he was faithful to God.

The greater the reputation of the leader, the greater the temptation is to allow personal power to corrupt.

Gideon's early faithfulness teaches us that with God on our side, victory is certain. His later failure is an example of the danger of replacing the divine agenda with our own personal ambition. The greater the reputation of the leader, the greater the temptation is to allow personal power to corrupt.

LESSON 7 EXAM

Use the answer sheet that has been provided to complete your exam.

1. **Gideon and his army of ___________ set up for the battle on the slopes of Mt. Gilead.**
   A. 300
   B. 3,000
   C. 23,000
   D. 32,000

2. **God told Gideon that his army was**
   A. too small.
   B. too large.
   C. poorly equipped.
   D. over-confident.

3. **This story illustrates the need for**
   A. adequate preparation in fighting battles.
   B. dependence on God in spiritual warfare.
   C. gathering our forces before the battle.
   D. encouraging others to stay faithful.

4. **The army that God approved to face the Midianites was outnumbered**
   A. 37 to 1.
   B. 43 to 1.
   C. 104 to 1.
   D. 443 to 1.

5. **The Lord further encouraged Gideon by**
   A. revealing the long-range results of the coming battle.
   B. showing him the large army of angels surrounding his soldiers.
   C. sending him to the enemy camp to hear their interpretation of a dream.
   D. bringing the high priest of Israel to stand by him.

6. **Gideon's response to the Lord's dealing with his fear was**
   A. worship.
   B. self-confidence.
   C. anxiety.
   D. indifference.

7. **The weapons for the battle were**
   A. catapults and swords.
   B. slings and stones.
   C. trumpets and clay jars.
   D. arrows and spears.

8. Gideon quieted the angry complaint of the Ephraimites by

A. answering back in anger.
B. ignoring them.
C. giving a gentle answer.
D. delaying answering them.

9. Gideon understood that Israel's government at that time was to be a

A. democracy.
B. theocracy.
C. republic.
D. monarchy.

10. The golden ephod that Gideon made became

A. a symbol of God's victory over the Midianites.
B. an expression of God's faithfulness.
C. a reminder of Gideon's strength.
D. an idol worshiped by the Israelites.

What Do You Say?

Why did Gideon fail to lead the people properly as time went on? How is this a warning for you?

LESSON 8

The Struggle to Have a Human King

Judges 9:1–10:18

After the death of Gideon, the children of Israel again were unfaithful to God by worshipping idols. In particular they made Baal-Berith their god and built a temple in his honor at the ancient religious city of Shechem (8:33; 9:46; cf. Gen. 12:6-7).

The record passes on to one of Gideon's sons, Abimelech, who made himself a king by conspiracy, started a civil war, and then ruled badly for three years. He finally died a humiliating death at God's hand. The story may seem out of place in the book because Abimelech was neither a judge nor a deliverer. But there are good reasons for its inclusion because it develops the main theme of the book, which is God's faithfulness to His covenant in the face of His people's unfaithfulness. In addition to the development of the book's theme, the story of Abimelech is …

- a testimony to the growing desire for a human king in Israel to replace Yahweh, their divine King. Gideon had refused to be a king, but he had edged closer to being one by his luxurious lifestyle (8:22-23, 29-30). Now, one of his sons conspired to be king. The concept of kingship was taking root among the people.
- an example of the development of Baal worship in the land. This idolatry was centered in Shechem, just twelve miles north of Shiloh, where the tabernacle of Yahweh's presence was located. It was a blatant affront to Yahweh.
- … is a description of the spiritual conditions in the central area of the land around Shechem. The other stories in Judges describe life in the south (Othniel and Ehud), north (Deborah and Barak),

east and north (Gideon), and west (Samson). It provides a number of practical lessons that alert God's people to dangers that result from ungodly conduct.

Abimelech Made King in Shechem (9:1-15)

Abimelech was one of Gideon's seventy sons. His mother was a concubine who lived in Shechem. Evidently he was brought up in princely lifestyle with all of Gideon's sons in Ophrah. Abimelech went to Shechem and implied that the sons of Gideon were intending to rule the land by some plan of their own. Abimelech took the opportunity to seize power for himself by persuading his mother's relatives in Shechem to help him become king. They were to influence the local leaders that he, as the only one of Gideon's sons who was related to them by blood, should be king.

He further incited them by referring to Gideon as "Jerubbaal," or "Baal fighter," in a city that was a center of Baal worship. He persuaded the city leaders that it would be advantageous to have a blood relative as their king. They gave him money from the temple of Baal. With that money Abimelech hired some scoundrels to go to Ophrah and assassinate his sixty-nine brothers. It was a mass murder "on one stone." These half brothers were simply citizens who had not made any move toward political advancement, nor even tried to become leaders. One of them, however—Gideon's youngest son, Jotham—had hidden himself and managed to escape.

Israel had become discontented and wanted a human king such as the Canaanites had.

Abimelech believed that he had eliminated the opposition and returned to Shechem to arrange a coronation ceremony for himself. He would be king over Shechem and three nearby towns, Beth-Millo, Arumah, and Thebez (9:41, 50). He did not know that Jotham had followed him to Shechem. During the coronation ceremony Jotham appeared on Mount Gerazim in full view of the city and the ceremony. His position on the mountain was an effective pulpit in a natural amphitheater. He soon had the attention of the coronation crowd, and he shouted out a parable, which was really a fable. It was a protest of the murder of his brothers and the foolishness of the people of Shechem to crown Abimelech as a king. Jotham was calling the Shechemites to account before God. He said in effect, "Listen to me ... that God may listen to what you have to say when you crown this worthless man as your king" (v. 7).

The parable was about trees that decided to anoint a king to reign over them. One tree after another declined the offer to "sway over [other] trees" because they were content to fulfill the purpose God had designed for them. The olive tree declined because its purpose was to give oil to honor God and men (vv. 8-9). The fig tree declined because its purpose was to bear sweetness and fruit (vv. 10-11). The vine declined because its purpose was to provide wine to cheer both God and men (vv. 12-13).

Finally all the trees turned to the bramble to be their king. The bramble is a useless plant that produces nothing of value. It bears no fruit, nor is its wood any use for building or even burning. It provides neither shade nor protection from the sun. Even worse, its fast growth suffocates other crops and is a menace to farmers. The bramble is also covered with thorns. When it dries out in the summer it feeds wild fires that spread very quickly and can destroy other crops (vv. 14-15). The bramble was a product of the curse of God because of sin. Yet the amazing thing is that "all the trees" wanted a king over them, even if it was a bramble. The bramble readily agreed and invited all the trees to come and take shelter under its shade. Then the bramble threatened them with a curse if they would not come under its rule. It said, "Let fire come out of the bramble and devour the cedars of Lebanon."

Jotham Interprets His Parable (9:16-21)

The trees represented the Israelites. God had placed them in the land to be fruitful like the olive, the fig, and the vine. But they had become discontented and wanted a human king such as the Canaanites had. So they were now ready to appoint a bramble-like person such as Abimelech to be their king. Jotham then interpreted his parable directly to the people at the coronation. He told them that just as the trees were unwise in trying to make the bramble their king, so they were unwise in making Abimelech their king. Then he challenged them to consider the background of what they were doing. He asked whether Abimelech's father, Gideon, had done anything to deserve the terrible assassination of all his sons by Abimelech. He reminded them that Gideon had actually risked his life to deliver them from the Midianites (v. 17).

He went on to rebuke them for their ingratitude to Gideon and their wickedness in murdering his sons, and their foolishness in making Abimelech the king of Shechem. The point of the story is that the people had rejected the rule of God and wanted a king like themselves to rule over them. So they appointed a worthless man to be king.

To conclude his warning against them, Jotham sarcastically told them that if what they were doing was right, they should now rejoice in their decision. But, he warned them that if what they were doing was wrong then they would be cursed. He said, "Let fire come out from Abimelech and devour the leaders of Shechem and Beth-millo; and let fire come out from the leaders of Shechem and from Beth-millo and devour Abimelech" (v. 20). Just as his parable had ended with fire coming from the bramble to destroy the cedars of Lebanon, so the interpretation ended with the prophetic warning, or curse, that fire would come from their new king to destroy them, and fire would come from them to destroy him (vv. 15, 20).

Jotham then noticed some men climbing toward him on the mountain where he was standing. Being fearful, he ran away to a safe place known as Beer, meaning "a well" (v. 21). Jotham is an example of godly steadfastness when, as the only son of Gideon left alive, he boldly stood up for righteousness, publicly opposing wrong, at the risk of his life.

The Spirit of Revolt in Shechem (9:22-25)

Abimelech ruled Shechem as king for three years, during which time God sent an evil spirit of distrust and jealousy between Abimelech and the Shechemites. The men of Shechem then tried to undermine Abimelech's government by limiting the income from tolls on the two caravan routes through the city. One went north/south and the other went east/west. They set bandits on them to raid the caravans and stop the travelers from passing through. In this way they soon ruined the economy of the city. It is interesting to reflect on God's action in sending an evil spirit (a demon) to accomplish this. Even demons are subject to the sovereign control of God (cf. Job 1:12; 2:6).

Gaal Leads the Revolt (9:26-29)

Abimelech reigned with an iron hand. Because of his unpopularity he appointed a man named Zebul to be his governor in Shechem and moved to the town of Arumah, five miles southeast (9:4, 30). Then a Canaanite man called Gaal moved into Shechem with a private army called "his brothers." Being a Canaanite, he disliked Abimelech the Israelite. Gaal sensed that there was growing dislike for Abimelech in Shechem and hoped to capitalize on it and become king himself. He ridiculed Abimelech and thought he had the support of the people. The people of Shechem began to put their confidence in Gaal (v. 26).

He made his move at the grape harvest festival in June/July when the people of the city were merry with wine. He led them in cursing Abimelech the Israelite, and the local governor, Zebul. They would be far better off, he said, if they had a Canaanite ruler and were faithful to the Canaanite heritage of the land. He reminded them of their ancestor Hamor whose son had raped Dinah, the daughter of Jacob, which resulted in both Hamor and his son Shechem being murdered by Simeon and Levi (Gen. 34:2, 26). Gaal implied that Abimelech should not rule Shechem because he was not from pure Canaanite stock. He told them that if he were ruler he would remove Abimelech. He challenged Abimelech to call out his army, thinking that he would easily defeat him (v. 29).

The Battle with Abimelech (9:30-49)

When Gaal challenged Abimelech to a battle, he misjudged how loyal Zebul would be to his master. Zebul sent a quick and secret message to Abimelech that he should muster his army that very night and secretly surround the city of Shechem. Then in the morning when the gates were opened and Gaal came out with his followers, they could be defeated easily. Abimelech followed this advice and surrounded the city that night (v. 34). In the morning Zebul and Gaal were both together looking out of the gate. Gaal saw Abimelech's men moving on the mountainside, but Zebul said they were only shadows (v. 36). When it became clear that they were under attack, Zebul challenged Gaal to go and attack them as he boasted he would the day before (v. 38). Gaal went out of the city with his men to fight, but his men were outnumbered and fled back to the city. Many were killed. By this time Zebul had mustered his own men in the city and forced Gaal and his men away from Shechem (v. 41).

Even demons are subject to the sovereign control of God.

Abimelech was still angry because of the rebellion in Shechem, and the next day he attacked the city again. He breached its walls and killed the people inside as well as those who fled. The leading men of the city tried to escape by hiding in the tower. It was a temple fortress in the inner city, also called the temple of Baal-Berith. Scholars think it was probably the same as the house of Millo (cf. 9:6, 20, 47, 49). Abimelech then went out and cut down the bough of a tree and told his men to do the same.

They took all these branches to the tower and piled them around it and set them alight. By doing this, a thousand people in the temple fortress of Baal died in the fire (vv. 45-49). In this way the prophetic curse of Jotham was fulfilled and "fire came out of the bramble" to destroy Shechem (cf. vv. 15, 20). Abimelech was the "bramble" who had now destroyed the city.

The Death of Abimelech (9:50-57)

Abimelech then went against the city of Thebez and captured it. It was ten miles northeast of Shechem and probably had joined in the revolt against him. He tried the same tactic as he had used in Shechem when the people fled for safety to the tower there. Abimelech came near to set the fire. Then a woman who had taken a millstone high in the tower dropped it on Abimelech's head. His skull was cracked, and as he lay dying he called on his armor-bearer to kill him with a sword so that it would not be said that a woman had killed him. Abimelech's followers saw that he was dead and they went home. In this way God repaid the wickedness that Abimelech had done to Gideon. Also, God had made the men of Shechem pay for their wickedness, fulfilling the curse of Jotham. Not only had fire from the "bramble" destroyed Shechem, but fire had come out of Shechem and consumed Abimelech, the bramble (cf. v. 20).

The final two verses in chapter 9 tell us that it was God who caused Abimelech to reap what he had sown when he dishonored his father and killed his brothers. And it was God who caused the men of Shechem also to reap the evil they had sown at Thebez. In this way the curse of Jotham was fulfilled (vv. 56-57).

Two "Lesser" Judges: Tola and Jair (10:1-5)

In the times of the judges, the periods of peace are dealt with in very few words. Usually there has been a simple statement, "The land had rest for … years" (cf. 3:11, 30; 5:31; 8:28). Two judges, Tola and Jair, are said to have risen up "to save Israel" after Abimelech. At the end of his unrighteous rule, the Israelites were ready for better leaders.

Tola, the Man from Issachar (10:1-2)

Tola is often referred to as a "minor" judge because only two verses are recorded about him. His name means "worm" and he came from a well-known family in the tribe of Issachar, located to the north of Ephraim's territory. He lived in the town of Shamir in the mountains of Ephraim. Men of Issachar were noted for their wisdom (1 Chron. 12:32). He arose to save Israel, which in this case indicates a preserving of its existence. Tola is presented as a leader who ruled quietly and effectively for twenty-three years.

Jair, the Gileadite (10:3-5)

Following Tola came Jair from Gilead. He governed God's people as their judge for the next twenty-two years. Gilead was east of the Jordan where the tribes of Reuben, Gad, and half the tribe of Manasseh had settled (Num. 32:41; Deut. 3:14). Jair was the descendant of another Jair who had taken several villages along the northern border of Gilead, near Bashan, and named them Havvoth-jair, which means "encampments of Jair" (Deut. 3:13; Num. 32:41; Josh. 13:30). From the statement that he had thirty sons we presume that he must have been a man of considerable stature and prosperity. They rode on thirty donkeys, meaning that they were distinguished by their rank. Each of the thirty sons was responsible for governing a city (1 Chron. 2:22; Josh. 13:30; 1 Kings 4:13). As in the case of Tola before him, he seems to have kept the nation in peace.

The Oppression by the Ammonites and the Philistines (10:6-9)

After the relative peace during the governances of Tola and Jair, the Israelites once again slipped back into the evil of idolatry. They "served the Baals and the Ashtaroth" and they "forsook the LORD." They illustrate the principle that if we don't learn the lessons of history—even our own history—we are doomed to repeat them. Israel succumbed to the attraction of the physical, sensual, and visible forms of religion that characterized Canaanite idolatry. They repeatedly broke the first and second commandments, in which God had forbade them to worship any gods other than Himself or to create any material idols (Ex. 20:1-6). For their unfaithfulness, God once again disciplined them this time by selling them into the hands of the Philistines on the west and the Ammonites on the east. They were caught between these two nations for eighteen long years. The worst of the pressure came from the Ammonites on the east side of the Jordan, who even crossed the Jordan and harassed the tribal areas of Ephraim, Benjamin, and Judah.

The Confession of the Israelites (10:10-18)

Observe the change in the Israelites' attitude at this point in the narrative. The Israelites confessed both types of sin that we identified in verse 6, saying, "We have forsaken our God" and "served the Baals." The Lord answered them by reciting some past deliverances from …

- the Egyptians at the Red Sea (Ex. 14:26-30)
- the Amorites in the Battle of Jahaz (Deut. 2:36-37)
- the Ammonites and Moabites in the Battle of Edrei (Deut. 3:1-11)
- the Philistines under Shamgar (3:31)
- the Sidonians, perhaps under Jabin and Sisera (4:12 ff)
- the Amalekites (6:3) and the Maonites, or Midianites (7:12)

The Lord then named their two sins again, "You have forsaken Me and served other gods" (v. 13). He wanted them to confess how powerless these gods really were. So He continued, " Go and cry out to the gods whom you have chosen; let them save you in the time of your distress." When the Lord challenged them a second time, it forced the Israelites to examine their hearts more deeply. Again they confessed their sin. They said, "We have sinned; do to us whatever seems good to you. Only please deliver us this day" (v. 15). This was the first time in the book of Judges that Israelites confessed they had sinned. The Lord had not yet promised deliverance, but the text records that they " put away the foreign gods from among them and served the LORD." Note that they rectified the two named sins that had plagued them (vv. 6, 10, 13, 16). Then it says of God that "He became impatient over the misery of Israel" (v. 16). It means that He felt their sufferings so deeply that in His compassion He delivered them. Though He had said, "I will save you no more," He reached out to them in mercy once again (v. 13). *That is grace!* It reveals the tension God faced between His love for Israel and the need to discipline them.

This was the first time in the book of Judges that Israelites confessed they had sinned.

The final two verses in this chapter introduce the battle by which God did provide deliverance for His people. The Ammonites advanced into Gilead from the east and the Israelites responded by setting up a base at Mizpah. But the Israelites did not seek God's guidance; instead they looked for a human leader. They promised that this human leader would be head over Gilead if he would agree to lead the army and defeat the Ammonites.

In doing this they were already saying "No" to the Lord's authority. They would soon find that their leader had some glaring weaknesses.

This chapter has some important contributions to make.

- In the theme of the development toward monarchy, this chapter details the first attempt to set up a monarchy in Israel. It failed.
- In the theme of growing apostasy in Israel, during the time of the judges, we note that the seeds of moral decay in Gideon's lifetime had now borne fruit in life of his son Abimelech. Both he and the city he ruled reaped what they had sown.

When Israel tried to "fix the problem" without bringing God into the equation they only brought further judgment on themselves. The lust for power, so evident in Abimelech's life, led him to ruthless tyranny, accusations about his brothers, and their murder. In the spiritual life of the believer, the flesh (sinful nature) wants to dominate, and the results are always destructive in nature. When we make the conscious choice to conduct our lives under the control of the indwelling Spirit of God, we will not fulfill the destructive desires of our sinful nature (Gal. 5:16).

LESSON 8 EXAM

Use the answer sheet that has been provided to complete your exam.

1. **The story of Abimelech is included in the book of Judges because**
   A. it develops the theme of God's faithfulness to His covenant.
   B. Abimelech was the most important of the judges.
   C. it shows the faithfulness of Israel.
   D. Abimelech led all the tribes of Israel for 40 years.

2. **After the murder of his brothers, Abimelech had himself proclaimed ____________ over Shechem and three other cities.**
   A. priest
   B. judge
   C. king
   D. prophet

3. **The point of Jotham's parable was that**
   A. the Canaanites from the north would attack and subjugate the city of Shechem.
   B. God would take revenge for the murder of Gideon's sons.
   C. the people had rejected the rule of God and wanted a human king.
   D. Abimelech would be a productive and loyal leader.

4. **The prophetic curse of Jotham was fulfilled when**
   A. Abimelech destroyed the city of Shechem.
   B. Gaal attacked Abimelech.
   C. Abimelech defeated Gaal.
   D. Zebal defected from Abimelech.

5. **Jair the Gileadite's prosperity and influence is indicated by his having**
   A. a large following of the local people.
   B. 30 sons who ruled 30 cities.
   C. an army to fight the Philistines.
   D. many farms and businesses.

6. The Israelites continually returned to the idolatry of Canaan because

A. they were forced to by their neighbors.
B. they thought God had forsaken them.
C. they were afraid of alienating the gods of the land.
D. they were drawn to the visible worship of gods they could see.

7. For their sin of idolatry, God sold Israel into the hands of

A. the Philistines and the Ammonites.
B. the Moabites and the Ammonites.
C. the Hivites and the Amorites.
D. the Jebusites and the Philistines.

8. For the first time recorded in the book, the Israelites

A. grew hostile to God's discipline.
B. admitted their sin.
C. denied that God existed.
D. blended completely into the Canaanite culture.

9. The seeds of moral decay in Gideon's lifetime

A. were uprooted by the influence of his compatriots.
B. had no particular effect on future generations.
C. bore fruit in the life of his son Abimelech.
D. were easily destroyed by his descendants.

10. In the life of the Christian,

A. the indwelling Holy Spirit always has victory over the flesh.
B. the flesh destroys the work of the Holy Spirit.
C. the desires of the flesh are eliminated by the Spirit.
D. walking under the control of the Spirit results in not carrying out the flesh's desires.

What Do You Say?

How does the account of Abimelech develop the theme(s) of the book of Judges?

LESSON 9

The Man Nobody Wanted

Judges 11:1–12:15

The Man Nobody Wanted (11:1-3)

Chapter 10 closes with the Israelites desperately looking for a military leader to help them fight against the people of Ammon. Evidently none of the existing leaders had any experience in war or the confidence of the people.

The first three verses of chapter 11 are a parenthesis in the narrative that informs us about the personal background of the next judge, Jephthah. No one would guess from his beginnings that he would be among the "heroes of faith" listed in Hebrews 11. Jephthah was born as the result of a sexual liaison between his father, Gilead, and a prostitute. Gilead and his legal wife raised Jephthah in their home and had other sons. But when the legitimate sons grew up they rejected him as a brother and excluded him from any inheritance. Jephthah fled to the northeast of Gilead to a place called Tob on the border between Ammon and Syria. He became a character like Robin Hood and developed skills in team leadership and attack strategy much as David did in the wilderness of Judah many years later. All this prepared him for his future leadership. In his rejection by his brothers and in his leadership of a band of outcasts, he is similar to Abimelech (cf. 8:31-9:4), though his character is much more righteous. He learned to know God; it is instructive to observe that as far as what is recorded in the inspired biblical narrative, Jephthah used the name of the Lord more than any other judge did. He and his men were

Jephthah learned to trust God.

social outcasts who formed themselves into a rogue band that lived well by raiding caravans of goods and travelers. In the bedouin culture their lifestyle would be respected, and Jephthah gained a reputation. In his preparation for leadership Jephthah learned three important things:

- He learned how to be a leader of men (v. 3).
- He learned the art of war to overcome his enemies (v. 3).
- He learned to know God (vv. 9-11).

Jephthah Called to be a Leader in Gilead (11:4-11)

Threatened by a war with Ammon and their need of a leader, the elders of Israel in Gilead put aside their dislike of Jephthah. They called him out of his exile to lead them against the enemy, recognizing that he was a gifted military leader. Once again God would use the unexpected person in unexpected ways to accomplish His purposes; He had done this with each of the preceding judges. Othniel was the original model, on whom the Spirit of God came so that he defeated the Mesopotamians and then judged Israel (3:10). But God did not follow that model in Ehud, the next judge. Instead His reason for choosing Ehud seemed to have been because he was left-handed and was able to use a hidden dagger to kill King Eglon. Then God surprised us again with Shamgar, who used an ox goad, a farm tool, to defeat the Philistines (3:31). He next surprises us by using Deborah, a woman prophetess whom He chose to gather the army and order the battle against the Canaanites. And then He finished the job with another woman, Jael, to kill Sisera, the Canaanite commander of Hazor.

Once again God would use the unexpected person in unexpected ways to accomplish His purposes.

Following these women, there was another surprise: Gideon, who was asked to pare down his army of 32,000 to 300. With them he defeated 135,000 Midianite invaders—but God wasn't finished with His surprises. He allowed Gideon's ruthless son, Abimelech, to rule as judge for three years as a tyrant, and then to die in humiliation as a result of the curse of Jotham (9:56-57). All of this simply says that God works in His own ways with all sorts of people.

When Jephthah was called to be the commander of the Gileadite army he showed his verbal skills in negotiating with them. Five short exchanges between him and the Gileadites drastically changed the whole situation. First, the Gileadites made an offer. "Come and be our leader, that we may fight against the Ammonites" (v. 6). He should have jumped at the chance to prove himself. His answer, however, was to take the advantage. He does not allow them to manipulate him. He said in effect, "You didn't want me before when you expelled me, but now you need me" (v. 7).

The elders' answer was to sweeten the offer because they did need him. They said, "Fight against Ammon" with us, and then be "our head" (our civil leader or tribal chief) afterwards (v. 8). Then Jephthah said in effect, "If you do it on my terms, then I will agree" (v. 9). Finally they accepted Jephthah's proposal. Jephthah and the elders then went to Mizpah and he was properly installed as both civil leader and military commander. Note Jephthah's negotiating skills in that he not only gained acceptance back into society, but also became their judge. Notice how he uses the name of the Lord in three ways: first, as the divine Deliverer, second, as the divine Adjudicator, and third, as the divine Witness (vv. 9-11).

Jephthah Negotiates with the King of Ammon (11:12-28)

Jephthah did not rush to battle to show the world what a powerful warrior he was, even though he was a rough-and-ready character. He first tried to settle the matter between the Gileadites and the Ammonites peacefully and truthfully. He sent messengers on a diplomatic mission to ask the King of Ammon why he was waging war against the Israelites (v. 12). The king must have been surprised that after eighteen years of oppressing the Israelites they were finally asking for a reason (cf. 10:8). The question was, "What do you have against me, that you have come to me to fight against my land?" (v. 12). Jephthah claimed that the land belonged to the Israelites. The Ammonite king wrote out a reply and sent it back to Jephthah.

Jephthah gives his reason for military action, saying, "Because Israel on coming up from Egypt took away my land, from the Arnon to the Jabbok ... Now therefore restore it peaceably" (v. 13). His answer contained several things that were not true, so Jephthah corrected him with the truth. Jephthah then answered that there were three reasons why the Ammonites had no claim on the land of Gilead:

- Historically, he reminded them that when Israel had taken over the land between the Arnon and the Jabbok Rivers, they had taken it from the Amorites under King Sihon and not from the Ammonites.

(Num. 21:21-24). The Amorites had previously taken it from the Ammonites (vv. 15-22).
- Theologically, he informed them that it was Yahweh who had given the Israelites that land, not the army of Israel (vv. 23-25). Even Canaanite peoples agreed that when a deity had given victory to the invaders, they had total rights over it. Jephthah lectured the Ammonite king that he should be content with what his god Chemosh had given him (v. 24). To highlight this point he said that even Balak, king of Moab in Moses' day, did not contest Israel's right to occupy the land (v. 25). Why then would the Ammonites contest it now?
- Logically, the Israelites had lived east of the Jordan for three hundred years since the days of Moses, from 1406 BC to 1106 BC. If the Ammonite claim was legitimate, they should have made it long ago (v. 26). Jephthah then summed up his arguments by saying, "I therefore have not sinned against you, and you do me wrong by making war on me" (v. 27).

Jephthah concluded by calling on "the LORD, the Judge," who held the rightful title to the land. He, the Lord, would render judgment in the matter between the Israelites and the Ammonites (v. 27). The phrase "The LORD, the Judge" is significant here and expresses a dominant theme in the book of Judges. In reply, the king of the Ammonites paid no attention to the words of Jephthah. He no doubt thought that he could easily win a battle against the Israelites led by a rough leader of highway raiders such as Jephthah. The Ammonite king then prepared for battle. But God had taken Jephthah from the "scrap heap" and enabled him to be a man He could use.

Jephthah Gathers an Army and Makes a Vow (11:29-31)

It was then that the Spirit of the Lord came upon, or clothed, Jephthah. This is the third time that it is recorded that the Spirit of the Lord came upon a judge in this book (the others being Othniel and Gideon). Now He comes upon Jephthah to enable him to defeat the Ammonites. The power of the Spirit did not make any of these men passive. It controlled them as they raised their armies, trained them, and developed a strategy for the coming battle. With the Spirit upon him, Jephthah recruited his soldiers in Gilead, east of the Jordan. He assembled and trained the recruits to become an army in the town of Mizpah where he now lived with his wife and daughter. Then he marched them east to face the Ammonite forces

(v. 29). The key to Jephthah's victory was that he was empowered by the Spirit of God. It would be God's victory, not Jephthah's.

Jephthah had the reputation of being a "mighty warrior" (v. 1). Now, just before the battle, he became aware that victory would only be his if the Lord was on his side. In order to assure himself of the blessing of God, he made a vow to God that sounds foolish to us. He promised God that if the Israelites were victorious in the battle, then whatever came out of the door of his home when he returned to Mizpah "shall be the LORD's, and I will offer it up for a burnt offering" (v. 31).

The key to Jephthah's victory was that he was empowered by the Spirit of God.

Bible commentators interpret what he meant by his vow differently. Some take it that if Jephthah defeated the Ammonites, the first person or animal that came out of his house when he came home would be taken to an altar (probably at the tabernacle in Shiloh) and be burned completely as a sacrifice in worship to God. Lambs had been offered morning and evening ever since God had given instructions to Moses on Mount Sinai about how the Israelites should worship. Other commentators understand that when Jephthah promised to offer it up as a burnt offering he was vowing to devote the person or animal that came out from his house completely to the Lord. More comment will follow on verses 34 to 40.

Jephthah's Victory (11:32-33)

The battle of Aroer is mentioned in just a few words. Jephthah attacked the Ammonites and the Lord delivered them into his hands. It was God's victory, and a great one at that. Twenty cities were destroyed from Aroer on the Arnon River in the south to Minnith and Abel Meramim, possibly near Rabbah. The emphasis is that the Lord who gave them their covenant blessed them in battle and gave them the victory.

Jephthah Keeps His Vow (11:34-40)

News of the victory had preceded Jephthah's return home to Mizpah. The people there welcomed him as a hero with great celebration. On his arrival home his daughter, his only child, came out to greet him with timbrels (tambourines) and dancing. When Jephthah saw her he remembered his vow and tore his clothes saying, "Alas, my daughter! You have brought me very low, and you have become the cause of great trouble to me. For I have opened my mouth to the LORD, and I cannot take back my vow" (v. 35).

His decision was based on his relationship to Yahweh. His daughter's answer states that she too believed that it was the Lord who gave her father victory and that she was willing to comply with the consequences of his promise. Then she requested he give her permission to spend two months with her companions to lament her virginity (that is, that she would never marry or have children). He agreed, and she did so. The scene closes when she returned to her father and he carried out the vow. The narrator's comment was, "She had never known a man, and it became a custom in Israel that the daughters of Israel went year by year to lament the daughter of Jephthah" (vv. 39-40). The reader is left with the question that when Jephthah carried out his vow, what exactly did he do to her?

- Did he sacrifice her on an altar as the pagan Canaanites did (2 Kings 3:27; 16:3; 21:6)?
- Or did he devote her to the Lord for a life of service in the tabernacle as a celibate woman?

There are arguments for both of these positions. But it is best to take it that his vow had nothing to do with human sacrifice, but was fulfilled in her devotion to a celibate life of service of God, for the following reasons:

- Jephthah would have known that God in His law had clearly forbidden the pagan practice of human sacrifice (Lev. 18:21; Deut. 18:10).
- Jephthah's high level of reverence for Yahweh argues against a vow of human sacrifice. There are seven references to the Lord in verses 9 to 32. Note especially that his negotiations with the Ammonites were made "before the LORD" (v. 11), the Spirit of the Lord came upon him (v. 29), his vow was made "to the Lord" (v. 30), and he kept his vow even in personal pain because he had given his "word to the LORD" (v. 35). The Bible honors him. Samuel honored him at the coronation of King Saul (1 Sam. 12:11), and he is among the "heroes of faith" listed in Hebrews 11:32.
- Jephthah's daughter clearly was brought up to honor God above her own desires (v. 36).
- It seems from Exodus 38:8 that women did serve at the tabernacle. Their work probably included washing and mending priestly clothes, and cleaning the area. The context for Jephthah's daughter was all about her virginity (vv. 37-39), not about her life, and fits well with a life that would have been devoted to service at the tabernacle.

- There is no explicit mention of her sacrifice by death in the passage. The phrase "offer it up for a burnt offering" usually refers to animal sacrifice on the altar, but was this what Jephthah really meant? Only a "clean" animal would have been acceptable as a sacrifice, anyway—he could not, after all, have sacrificed something like a dog to God.

Ephraim's Complaint to Jephthah (12:1-7)

The people of the sizeable tribe of Ephraim were troublemakers. They were Gilead's neighbors to the west. Some years earlier, when Gideon was at war with the Midianites, they refused to help him in the final phases of the battle because they were jealous of his victory. They complained after the main battle that they had not been invited, and only Gideon's diplomacy saved the day. Now this current generation complained after Jephthah's battle with the Ammonites was over, saying that Jephthah had not invited them to help. They threatened to set fire to Jephthah's house (v. 1). The truth was that the Ammonites had been harassing Gilead for fifteen years and the Ephraimites had not lifted a finger to help them. Jephthah replied that he had indeed called them to help, but they had not responded (vv. 1, 3). But the Lord had given him the victory even without the Ephraimites.

The Ephraimites then turned hostile and mustered an army to fight Jephthah at Mizpah. Jephthah learned they were coming and moved to meet them at Zaphon near the Jordan. War broke out there and Jephthah's well-trained troops easily won the day. He knew that the Ephraimites in retreat would have to cross the fords of the Jordan to get home. So he stationed his men there to ask all those who wanted to cross to say the word *shibboleth,* which means "flowing stream." The Ephraimites could not pronounce the word using the "sh," but used an "s"; they would say *sibboleth* instead. Thus they were easily identified as Ephraimites and killed on the spot. A total of 42,000 were thus killed. The whole scene, with Israelites killing Israelites because of pride and jealousy, was a sad chapter in their history.

But the Lord had given him the victory.

The word "shibboleth" has come to mean something that distinguishes one group from another. How often factions in churches or groups of churches have fought to their great harm over issues stemming from pride and jealousy. They often use some "litmus test" by which to judge their brethren. Great people have often displayed great flaws as did Jephthah when he continued the war against the Ephraimites. He had benefited from the grace of God, but did not treat others with grace.

Jephthah's reputation as a leader grew after the battle and he went on to judge Israel, at least the Trans-Jordanian tribes, for six years. He was eventually buried in Gilead (v. 7). Both his accomplishments and his mistakes are helpful examples to us.

Ibzan, Elan, and Abdon (12:8-15)

Another group of "minor" judges are listed after Jephthah. Their leadership may overlap others. Ibzan judged in Bethlehem in the south, Elon in Zebulun in the north, and Abdon in Pirathon an Ephramite city in the center of the land.

Ibzan (12:8-10)

Ibzan was probably from the tribe of Judah as he both served and was buried in Bethlehem. He must have been wealthy, with multiple wives, indicated by thirty sons and thirty daughters. This is in contrast to Jephthah, who had one wife. He seems to have extended his influence and alliances by having his sons and daughters marry influential partners from distant places. He was the first judge in Judah since Othniel some three hundred years before. He judged for seven years.

Elon (12:11-12)

Elon judged in the Galilee region in the territory of Zebulun. He judged Israel for ten years. Zebulun had been involved with Deborah and Barak, and later with Gideon.

Abdon (12:13-15)

Abdon, too, had a large family. The fact that they rode on young donkeys is probably an indication of some wealth and position. He judged Israel for eight years.

LESSON 9 EXAM

Use the answer sheet that has been provided to complete your exam.

1. **Jephthah fled to Tob because**
   A. his brothers threatened to kill him.
   B. he had murdered his brothers.
   C. his brothers rejected him.
   D. the community was under attack.

2. **During his time of exile, Jephthah**
   A. learned to know God.
   B. made frequent attacks on his father's house.
   C. pursued the worship of Baal.
   D. lived alone in the desert.

3. **When Jephthah was installed as the leader of the Gileadites he**
   A. sent messengers on a diplomatic mission to the king of Ammon.
   B. immediately attacked the Ammonites.
   C. ignored the threat of war with the Ammonites.
   D. spent time solidifying his power.

4. **The phrase Jephthah uses of God, "the Lord, the Judge,"**
   A. expresses a minor theme of the book.
   B. expresses a dominant theme in the book.
   C. is the main theme of the book.
   D. is the one and only theme of the book.

5. **Jephthah was victorious in the battle because**
   A. his soldiers were well trained.
   B. he was an understanding leader.
   C. he was controlled by the Spirit of God.
   D. he was determined to retain his power.

6. Jephthah vowed that if the Israelites won the battle he would (when he returned home)

A. give a large donation to the priests at the tabernacle.
B. always worship only Jehovah.
C. offer as a burnt offering whatever first came out of his house.
D. rule the people with kindness and justice.

7. Jephthah's initial response to how he was going to fulfill his vow was one of

A. relief.
B. distress.
C. anger.
D. enthusiasm.

8. In understanding what Jephthah meant by his vow, we should take into account

A. the honor with which Jephthah is held in other Scriptures.
B. God's clear condemnation of human sacrifice in the law.
C. the emphasis in the text on the issue of his daughter's virginity.
D. all of the above.

9. After the battle with the Ammonites, the tribe of Ephraim

A. praised Jephthah for his victory.
B. celebrated the victory with the Gileadites.
C. asked Jephthah to rule over them.
D. complained that they had not been invited to help.

10. The Ephraimites were easily identified because they

A. had distinctive facial features.
B. could not pronounce the "sh" sound.
C. were all left-handed.
D. spoke with a different dialect.

What Do You Say?

Identify Jephthah's good and bad qualities. What lessons can you learn from him?

LESSON 10

Samson, Empowered by the Spirit

Judges 13:1–14:20

Chapter 13 begins the sixth of the downward cycles in the book. These followed Israel's disobedience, departure, discipline, and deliverance. In this section, the major enemy was Philistia and the deliverer was Samson. The Philistines built a confederacy of five powerful city-states: Gaza, Ashkelon, Ashdod, Ekron, and Gath. They oppressed Israel's southern tribes for forty years, the longest oppression recorded in Judges. The oppression began about the same time as Jephthah was delivering the tribes east of Jordan from the Ammonites (c. 1095 BC).

Reasons for Oppression from the Philistines (13:1)

The *spiritual reason* for the Philistine oppression was that the Israelites had offended the Lord by adopting the pagan worship of the Philistine god, Dagon. The *economic reason* was that the Philistines controlled Israel's economy with a monopoly on agricultural land and iron implements. The *military reason* was the superiority of their iron weapons over the bronze weapons of Israel. And the *social reason* was that the Israelite intermarriage with the Philistines blurred the differences between them. The result was that the Israelites again left God out of their lives, adopted the religion of the Philistines, and accepted their economic oppression as normal. The result was that "the LORD gave them into the hand of the Philistines" (13:1). Their situation illustrates what is happening in Christendom today. Many are forsaking the true God and being seduced by post-modern culture, offering no resistance. They are accepting it all as normative. Like the proverbial frog in the kettle, they are slowly dying without realizing it.

Samson, God's Deliverer

In contrast to their response in the former "cycles," in this instance the Israelites did not repent from their sin or cry out to God before He took steps to save them. God acted in grace in providing Samson as their deliverer this time. Unlike previous judges, Samson did not raise an army. He fought alone against the Philistines to hold back their gradual assimilation of Israel. He was God's man for the times even though his personal failures and undisciplined weaknesses resulted in tragedy and his early death. Samson's short life is usually seen as an illustration of the dangers of compromise. We also need to remember, however, that the Scripture's own commentary on Samson is not a warning about the danger of lust but an encouragement to act in God's strength as Samson did when he "stopped the mouths of lions" (Heb. 11:32-33).

Samson's life demonstrates that God sometimes uses badly-flawed leaders to accomplish His sovereign purposes.

God used Samson to "begin to save Israel" from the oppression of the Philistines. Deliverance from Philistine power was finally accomplished at the battle of Mizpah, which was led by Samuel after Samson's death (v. 5; 1 Sam. 7:2-12). Samson's life also demonstrates, once again, that God sometimes uses badly-flawed leaders to accomplish His sovereign purposes. However that may be, we can still learn some great lessons of faith from him. It is significant that the Holy Spirit, in inspiring what was recorded in Scripture, gives more space to Samson as a deliverer of God's people than to any other judge.

Conditions in the Tribal Area of Dan

Samson was from the tribe of Dan that had been very influential during the wilderness journey. In Canaan, Joshua had assigned them territory west of Benjamin, but they failed to secure it from the Amorites. Most of them then fled northward to Laish, north of Galilee. Then around 1200 BC increasing numbers of Philistines came by sea from the Aegean. These new enemies gradually dominated the coastal plain. Danites like Samson's parents were forced to live in the hills and eke out a living (1:34; 18:29). Dan thus became the least influential of all the tribes, without a single walled city in which they could defend themselves. Manoah and his wife lived in the village of Zorah near the border of Philistine territory about fourteen miles west of Jerusalem. To their sorrow, they had no children.

The Angel's Announcement of Samson's Birth (13:2-5)

The Angel of the Lord suddenly appeared to Manoah's wife and reminded her that she was barren and had no children. Then He announced to her that she would conceive and bear a son (v. 3). He went on to instruct her not to drink wine or alcohol during her pregnancy because her son would be a "Nazirite to God" from his conception.

The word *Nazirite* is from the Hebrew word "Nazir" and carries with it the idea of separation and dedication. A Nazirite under the Mosaic Law was one who voluntarily took a vow of separation from life's ordinary duties and devoted himself to God, usually for a limited time and for a specific purpose. The "Law of the Nazirites" is described in Numbers 6. But in the case of the son to be born to Manoah and his wife, his dedication was to be lifelong. He would be required to keep certain rules in order to be holy (separated) to the Lord (v. 8). He was to …

- abstain from consuming any fermented drink (v. 4; Num. 6:3-4). This would enable him to have a clear mind to concentrate on accomplishing God's purpose for him.
- abstain from cutting his hair (v. 5; Num. 6:5). His uncut hair would indicate to all his Nazarite status.
- abstain from any contact with a dead body (Num. 6:6). Touching nothing dead would indicate his separation from everything that was unclean.

Samson's Calling

Samson's God-given task as a Nazirite was to "begin to save Israel from the hand of the Philistines." He would start the process of delivering Israel by using his physical strength to reduce the oppression of the Philistines and to keep them from making further inroads into Israel. The Nazarite rule about not cutting his hair is included because it will impact the story of Samson's greatest deed. As believers we can learn from the Nazirite principle of separation. It illustrates that we, too, are called to be a separated people unto the Lord and characterized by personal holiness (1 Peter 1:16; 2 Cor. 7:1).

Manoah's Lesson about Faith and Obedience (13:6-14)

Manoah's wife hurried to share her news with him, though she could not identify her visitor. She told him that her visitor was a "man of God," a prophet, and that his face had appeared to her like the face of an angel. But she was so excited that she did not ask where he came from or what his name was. But she did not report to Manoah that God's purpose for their son was to begin to deliver Israel from the Philistines.

Manoah's response was to pray that Yahweh would send the "man of God" back to teach them what they should do for the child who was coming (vv. 8, 12). His prayer is a model prayer for parents who anticipate a new child in the home. He then assumed the spiritual leadership in the home. He asked for wisdom from God to raise the boy. God answered his prayer, but not exactly as he had asked. The man of God did return and appear again to Manoah's wife. She ran and told Manoah, who followed her back to where the Angel was. He asked the Angel if he was the man who spoke to his wife. The Angel answered, "I am" (v. 11).

Manoah's prayer is a model prayer for parents who anticipate a new child in the home.

Manoah then asked the Angel directly, "What is to be the child's manner of life, and what is his mission?" (v. 12). Note that the Angel does not answer his question. All He said was that He had already told Manoah's wife what to do: "Let her be careful … All that I commanded her let her observe" (vv. 13-14). What He had told her was that because the boy would be a Nazirite she should not drink wine while she carried Samson in her womb. The point for Manoah was that he should simply trust God and obey what he had been commanded, not keep asking for more details. The essence of faith is to accept and act upon what God reveals. Manoah learned the lesson and asked no more about the boy's future. We too should be careful to obey the revealed will of God in Scripture and not think we need to know all the details as they apply to us individually.

The Visitor Reveals His Identity (13:15-23)

Manoah still assumed that his visitor was an itinerant prophet. So he offered to prepare a meal for him as would be customary for an unexpected visitor. The Angel replied that He would not eat their food. But He said that if they prepared a burnt offering, they should offer it to Yahweh (v. 16). It began to dawn on Manoah that his Visitor might be more than a prophet. He asked Him directly, "What is your name?" thinking perhaps that he would "honor" Him with a gift when the promised son was born (v. 17).

The Angel's answer was most revealing and it brings the story to a climax. He said, "Why do you ask my name, seeing it is wonderful?" (v. 18). It was not the proper name of the Angel, but it expressed His character, His divine nature. He is absolutely and supremely wonderful. The Hebrew word indicates that the Angel's character is inscrutable, it is beyond understanding. The psalmist, when describing how much God knew about him, used the word this way: "Such knowledge is too wonderful for me" (Ps. 139:6). Hundreds of years later the prophet Isaiah used the term in describing the coming Messiah: "His name shall be called, 'Wonderful Counselor …'" (Isa. 9:6).

Then the next verse tells us that the Angel called "Wonderful" would do a "wondrous thing," using the same word. What was the "wondrous thing" that happened? Manoah offered a goat as a blood sacrifice together with a grain offering on an altar. As the flame of the offering was ascending to heaven the Angel ascended in it and was gone (v. 19). The wonder of it showed that the Angel of the Lord was indeed divine.

Manoah realized that he had been in God's presence. He and his wife fell on their faces to the ground and worshipped (vv. 20-21). The Angel who appeared to them was the One who had appeared to Hagar by the desert spring (Gen. 16:7-11). He was the One who called to Abraham on Mount Moriah (Gen 22:11-15). He was the One who appeared to Moses at the burning bush (Ex. 3:2). He was the One who also appeared to Gideon (6:12). Manoah then assumed that he and his wife would die because they had seen God, but his wife was more objective than he. She reasoned that they would not die, because the Lord had accepted their offering and promised that they would have a son (v. 23).

The essence of faith is to accept and act upon what God reveals.

The Birth of Samson (13:24-25)

Concerning the child's birth we are told simply that Manoah's wife bore a son and called his name Samson. Then concerning his early years we learn only that he grew and the Lord blessed him. At some point the family moved from Zorah to nearby Mahaneh Dan or Camp of Dan where it says that "the Spirit of the LORD began to stir him." Samson must have come to realize that he was not simply a physically strong man, but that he had an extraordinary ability by the power of the Spirit. This is the first of four references to the Spirit's activity in Samson, more than in any other judge (14:6, 19; 15:14).

A review of God's preparation for Samson in Judges 13 will show us that God had prepared him in an extraordinary way to serve Him:

- The Angel of the Lord announced his birth and mission (v. 3).
- His godly parents prayed for wisdom to raise him (v. 8).
- He was appointed as a Nazirite for life in dedication to God (v. 5).
- God commissioned him to begin to deliver Israel from Philistine oppression (v. 5).
- The Lord blessed him from his youth (v. 24).
- The Spirit of God anointed him to do exploits (v. 25).

God's Purpose Accomplished through Samson (14:1–16:31)

The remainder of the Samson epic consists of two sections centered in two geographical areas of Philistine territory. The first centers on events in the town of Timnah (14:1-15:20), and the second on the city of Gaza (16:1-31). Both sections include a great victory for Samson in which Samson is responsible for the death of thousands of Philistines. And both sections conclude with a statement about the twenty years that Samson judged Israel (15:20 and 16:31). In this way both sections confirm that Samson's life accomplished God's purpose of beginning to deliver Israel from the Philistines (13:5). But while the purpose of God was being accomplished through the events of his life, the undisciplined life of Samson himself was descending into chaos. It is an ever-present danger for every servant of God.

Samson's Wedding Plans in Timnah (14:1-4)

As the events now begin to unfold, Samson would have been roughly twenty years old. He knew from the announcement of the Angel to his mother that he was destined by God to begin to deliver Israel from the hand of the Philistines. He also knew that the Spirit of God had already begun to "move upon him" or "stir him" (13:25). Perhaps this led him to visit the town of Timnah in Philistine territory, only an hour's walk from Mahane Dan (Camp of Dan) where he was living.

However it was, Samson found himself in the Philistine town of Timnah. While there he was attracted to a beautiful girl of marriageable age. He fell in love with her and demanded that his parents "get her" for him as a wife. His judgment seems to be based on her appearance as he said, "I saw one of the daughters of the Philistines." Marriages to the pagans of

Canaan were forbidden to Israelites, God's covenant people. His parents were upset because they knew of God's purposes for him. The Lord chose Israel to be a people for Himself (Ex. 34:10-17; Deut. 7:1-6). The woman Samson wanted to marry was an unbeliever. Samson's parents called her a woman from the "uncircumcised Philistines" (v. 3). The same prohibition of marriage to an unbeliever applies to believers today (2 Cor. 6:14).

His parents rightly resisted his demand, asking him if there was no woman in all of Israel that he must marry a Philistine. Samson did not listen to them except to demand, "Get her for me, for she is right in my eyes." We might well imagine how hard it was for them. But they gave in and the next thing we read about them was that they were on their way to Timnah to arrange the wedding. What they did not know is that God was using Samson's selfish demands for His own purposes. He was opening the way for Samson to become the judge of Israel. So we read that, "It was from the LORD"—for he was seeking an opportunity against the Philistines (v. 4). This is the key to understanding the whole section from 14:1 to 15:20. God was working through Samson's weakness and sin to work out His plans and purposes. It does not excuse Samson for marrying the Philistine. He would ultimately pay a high price for doing so. But it does explain that God often works outside the boxes we construct in our minds. "How unsearchable are His judgments and how inscrutable His ways!" (Rom. 11:33).

The undisciplined life of Samson himself was descending into chaos.

Samson Kills a Lion (14:5-9)

Samson's parents eventually gave in to his demands and went to Timnah to arrange the wedding. While Samson was walking alone in the vineyards of Timnah a lion attacked him. The Spirit of God came on him and he easily tore the lion in pieces with his bare hands. It may have been the first time he used his super-human strength, but he told no one of the incident.

The arrangements for the wedding were made with the Philistine woman's family for she "was right in Samson's eyes" (v. 7). That phrase is literally, "pleased Samson." Later, at the arranged time, Samson returned to Timnah for the wedding itself. On his way he revisited the spot where he had killed the lion. He found a swarm of bees there, and their honey was in the carcass of the dead lion. He removed some of the honey to eat. When he joined his parents he gave some to them also, but he did not tell them where it came from, no doubt because he knew they would be upset that he had broken one of his Nazarite vows.

Samson's Riddle at the Wedding (14:10-20)

At the wedding Samson provided a seven-day feast in the bride's home. The bride's family invited thirty "companions" for Samson, thought by some to be more like military guards. Many commentators believe that the feast was a drinking party and that Samson was breaking his Nazirite obligation not to drink wine. But Scripture is silent on the subject, and we should not draw conclusions from silence.

As part of the entertainment at the wedding, Samson suggested he pose a riddle to his thirty "companions." If they were able to solve the riddle by the time the seven-day wedding feast was over, he would give each of them a prize. These garments as described in the text were status symbols in ancient cultures. Samson went on to say that if the thirty guests could not solve the riddle, they would have to give Samson thirty such garments. They accepted the challenge saying, "Put your riddle" (v. 13). Samson's riddle concerned the lion he had killed, and he said,

> Out of the eater came something to eat,
> And out of the strong came something sweet.

Samson knew that the riddle was next to impossible to solve, as they would not have known of the incident of his killing the lion and of the honey he had then found in its carcass. For three days the companions puzzled over the riddle without success. Then they accused Samson's wife and father-in-law of plotting against them. They commanded her to entice Samson to reveal the answer or she and her father would be burned with fire (v. 15). For the next four days she pleaded with Samson and accused him of not loving her. She pressed him with tears and nagging. He finally relented on the seventh day and told her of the lion and the honey and she immediately told the thirty men. They triumphantly brought the answer to Samson before the deadline (v. 18). They had cheated, and in his angry reply Samson said: "If you had not plowed with my heifer, you would not have found out my riddle."

In calling his wife "a heifer" Samson was accusing her of having an untamed and stubborn spirit (Hosea 4:16). His anger was more directed at his wife than at the thirty companions because it was she who had betrayed him.

Then for the second time it says, "And the Spirit of the LORD rushed upon him" (v. 19; cf. v. 6). The first time it was to enable him to kill the lion. Now it was to pay his debt and to demonstrate the power of his God. He went down to the coastal city of Ashkelon, twenty-three miles southwest of Timnah. There he killed thirty of their men and took their fine clothes as booty in an act of war. He was fulfilling his divinely given role as a judge of Israel. He carried the clothes back to Timnah and gave them to his thirty companions. He may have deliberately obtained them far away so that his companions would not know where they came from. Still angry, he left his wife in Timnah and went to his father's house, probably located in Zorah. He did not intend to abandon his wife but to allow time for his anger to subside because she had betrayed him. In the meantime, however, his bride's parents gave his wife to his companion who had been his best man (v. 20). For that, they would pay a high price (15:6).

God often works "outside the box."

God used the wedding event as an occasion to provoke the Philistines and to use their fear of Samson and his power to limit their oppression in Israel. But God would still hold Samson accountable for disobeying the marriage laws that He had given to his covenant people. Samson's weakness in disciplining himself regarding relations with the opposite sex would plague him during the entire twenty years of being a judge in Israel.

LESSON 10 EXAM

Use the answer sheet that has been provided to complete your exam.

1. **In Judges 13-16, the major enemies of Israel were**
   A. the Moabites.
   B. the Philistines.
   C. the Amorites.
   D. the Ammonites.

2. **God used Samson to begin to deliver the Israelites from this oppression**
   A. even though they had not cried out to Him for help .
   B. because they cried to Him.
   C. when they repented from their sin.
   D. because he was a righteous man.

3. **Manoah's wife was told that she would conceive and bear a son. This announcement came from**
   A. a prophet.
   B. a holy man.
   C. the angel Gabriel.
   D. the Angel of the Lord.

4. **A Nazirite was a person who was**
   A. born in the city of Nazareth.
   B. a freely elected ruler of Israel.
   C. separated from life's normal duties and devoted to God.
   D. sent as an ambassador to a foreign country.

5. **Manoah and his wife realized they had been in the presence of God when**
   A. the Angel told them He had come from heaven.
   B. the Angel enjoyed a meal they had prepared.
   C. the Angel ascended in the flame of their burnt offering.
   D. the Angel told them His name.

6. **Samson demanded that his parents**
   A. arrange his marriage to a Philistine woman.
   B. move to the Philistine city of Timnah.
   C. provide a large amount of money for his exploits.
   D. give a party for him and his friends.

7. **The fact that God was using Samson's selfish demands for a gentile wife to initiate an attack on the Philistines**
   A. proves that God can sometimes act deceitfully.
   B. illustrates that God's ways of working are beyond our understanding.
   C. excuses Samson from breaking this basic rule for any Israelite.
   D. shows us that marriages with unbelievers can sometimes have good results.

8. **During the wedding feast, Samson**
   A. challenged the guests to an athletic competition.
   B. bragged about his physical strength.
   C. explained about his Nazirite vow.
   D. posed a riddle about the lion he had killed.

9. **Samson was able to obtain 30 garments for the men at the wedding because**
   A. the Spirit of the Lord came upon him mightily.
   B. he received help from his family.
   C. the Israelites joined his attack on the Philistines.
   D. he was an honorable man who paid his debts.

10. **God used the wedding event as an occasion to**
   A. teach Samson a lesson.
   B. unite the Israelites and Philistines into one people.
   C. provoke the Philistines.
   D. teach us to tolerate marriages between believers and unbelievers.

What Do You Say?

How do you account for God choosing a man like Samson to do His work?

LESSON 11

Samson, Driven by Lust

Judges 15:1–16:31

The Israelites had been oppressed by the Philistines for forty years (13:1). They had compromised their covenant with the Lord by practicing idolatry and were now in the grip of the Philistines. But God in His grace had prepared a leader named Samson who would begin to save them from their oppressors. He would do it by several victories over the enemy and by demonstrating, as in the case of his predecessors, that one man empowered by God could make a difference. Like his fellow Hebrews, Samson was deeply affected by the decadent culture. But in spite of this, God used him in remarkable ways. In chapter 15 God used him to defeat the Philistines in three personal battles. And in chapter 16 he brought down the temple of Dagon, killing thousands.

Samson Claims His Wife (15:1-2)

Some months after the wedding feast in Timnah, Samson returned there to claim his wife. He brought a gift because he had left in anger (owing to her leaking the answer to his riddle). Her father, however, had given the bride to Samson's best man. He then offered Samson his younger daughter to try to placate him. Samson was deeply offended because of this further treachery. He then carried out a response that demonstrated the power of Israel's God over the Philistines. It proved to be another of the incidents against the Philistines that were "from the LORD" (cf. 14:4).

Foxes Destroy the Harvest (15:3-6)

Samson said, "This time I shall be innocent in regard to the Philistines, when I do them harm." He had been blamed for killing the thirty innocent men in Ashkelon so he could present his wedding companions with the clothing he had wagered (v. 3; cf. 14:18). This time the harm he caused was deserved on all sides. He went out into the fields, where God enabled him to catch three hundred foxes and tie them together in pairs, tail to tail. Then he attached a flaming torch between each pair and set them loose. Fires soon raged in the ripe fields, vineyards, and olive groves, burning up the major crops of the land at harvest time. The result was enormous damage to the economy of the Philistines over a wide area. When the lords of the Philistines demanded to know who did it, the answer was "Samson, the son-in-law of the Timnite, because he has taken his wife and given her to his companion."

Samson demonstrates that one man empowered by God could make a difference.

Samson's Revenge (15:7-8)

The Philistines were afraid of Samson, so they took out their frustration on Samson's wife and her father, burning them alive in their home. In doing this the Philistines further angered Samson, who evidently still loved the Timnite woman. But again, his revenge was limited. He attacked with a "great blow." In all of this, God was using Samson to demonstrate His power to the Philistines. After the attack he did not dare live at home in Zorah. He made his home in a cave in a cleft at the top of the rock Etam. Living there he could protect himself from his enemies.

Samson's Rejection by the Men of Judah (15:9-13)

In seeking Samson, the Philistines sent a large army to set up camp in Judah's territory and told the men of Judah that they had come to arrest, or bind, Samson. They wanted the men of Judah to capture him and bring him bound to them. The men of Judah were afraid of offending the Philistines and willing to take their side against Samson. So Judah sent three thousand men to the rock of Etam to persuade Samson to give himself up. They blamed him for putting them in danger saying, "Do you not know that the Philistines are rulers over us? What then is this that you have done to us?" (v. 11). They would rather live in bondage to their enemies than in a covenant relationship with God. They knew very well that God had given victory to Israel over the last three hundred years under the leadership of Othniel, Deborah, Gideon, and Jephthah. But these three thousand wanted to make their own decisions. They were willing to sacrifice Samson if the Philistines would go home quietly.

They made it clear that they had come to arrest Samson. Samson did not even argue with them. So in another demonstration of self-control he took the moral high ground of a true hero. He was even willing to die, but he made them promise not to kill him themselves.

The church today is composed of many who refuse to fight for the truth. They prefer to compromise rather than confront.

The church today is composed of many who refuse to fight for the truth. They are no better than the men of Judah. They prefer to compromise rather than confront. They don't want to offend the immoral lifestyle of their neighbor who lives with her boyfriend. They say nothing when the name of God is taken in vain. They shrug when churches appoint unqualified leaders, or when the media denies the deity of Christ. They are silent when God is removed from the public square and the schools. They do not protest the lie of evolution. They are afraid to challenge the status quo. They fear losing their reputation, or employment, or their comfortable lifestyle.

Samson's Victory at Lehi (15:14-17)

The men of Judah bound Samson with two new ropes and led him from the rock Etam to where the Philistines were at Lehi, a name meaning, "jawbone." When the Philistines saw him they let out a shout of triumph thinking that Samson was in their hands at last. But at that moment the Spirit of the Lord came mightily upon him. It is the fourth and last time that that the statement is made about Samson. Immediately he broke the new ropes on his arms when they became like burned flax; they broke loose as if they melted. Then Samson found the fresh jawbone of a donkey and used it as a weapon to kill one thousand Philistine soldiers. The power of the Spirit of God worked through him so that dead Philistines were piled up in heaps.

By this time Samson was desperately tired and thirsty, but holding the jawbone of the donkey in his hand he made up a catchy rhyme to celebrate the victory. It is really a play on the Hebrew word *hamor* that means both "donkey" and "heap." He said,

> With the jawbone of a donkey, heaps upon heaps;
> With the jawbone of a donkey have I struck down a thousand men.

To catch the play on words one translator has it: "With the jawbone of an ass, I have piled them in a mass." He said, in effect, "I have made asses of them." Actually, he had not only made asses of the Philistines, but also of his own countrymen who looked on and did nothing.

Samson's ditty expressed the wonder of what happened. In honor of the occasion he named the place "Ramath Lehi," which means the "hill of the jawbone." The whole drama is really a high point in Samson's life of faith. He had faith to be humble and meek when his cowardly countrymen asked him to submit to the Philistines. He had faith to attack the Philistine army with only the jawbone of a donkey. He had faith to give the Lord the glory for the victory when he prayed, "You have granted this great salvation by the hand of Your servant" (v. 18; Heb. 11:32).

Samson's Prayer for Water (15:18-19)

After such a long day's battle Samson was very dehydrated. In prayer he acknowledged God's victory that day, but was concerned for God's glory if he died in Philistine hands. God heard his prayer and opened a seam in the rock, and water came out. In thanksgiving, Samson called the name of the place "En Hakkore," which means "The spring of him who calls." It is a witness to the truth that God answers prayer about even temporal needs.

Samson as a Judge of Israel (15:20)

The dramatic events of chapters 14 and 15 had taken place over a period of a year or so. The Philistines were sufficiently fearful of Samson that they did not trouble Israel for a long time. The narrator then informs us that Samson "judged Israel twenty years." It does not say that the land had rest (cf. 3:11), for the Philistines were still in the land. During his first year of displaying his God-given strength, he gained enough respect from the Israelites and the Philistines that he could set up some sort of administration in the area of Dan and Judah. He acted as judge of the issues and disputes that arose, and as the administrator of economic, military, and political matters.

The question may be asked, how could Samson have been so self centered, so sensual, and so neglectful of God's law, and yet be a man of faith? The answer is that he was the cultural product of the backslidden Israelites in his time, just as believers today are influenced by the decadent culture of the modern world. A second question might be, how could God could use a person with the weakness and flaws that Samson had? The answer is that God is committed to fulfill His promises. The New Testament reminds us is that we have the treasure of His truth in earthen vessels (that is, *us*), so that the excellence of the power may be of God and not of us (2 Cor. 4:7).

Samson and the Harlot of Gaza (16:1-2)

The events recorded in chapter 16 occur when he had been a judge in Israel for nearly twenty years (15:20). We have no record of other events between those that ushered in his judgeship in chapter 15 and those that brought his judgeship and life to an end in chapter 16. We assume that the Philistines had given up their attempts to capture Samson, and that he, in turn, had stopped harassing the Philistines. There is no clear indication as to where he lived as judge though his home village of Zorah is suggested, or perhaps the city of Hebron in Judah (cf. v. 3).

In his twentieth year as a judge, Samson traveled to the Philistine city of Gaza. His journey there was probably for diplomatic reasons. Going to Gaza, a walled and fortified city, was extremely risky for him. He was public enemy number one to the Philistines; they were still looking for opportunities to capture him. But while there in Gaza he "saw a prostitute" and gave in to his own passions. Moral failure when traveling alone in a strange city has been the downfall of many Christian leaders.

Moral failure when traveling alone in a strange city has been the downfall of many Christian leaders.

Samson Carries away the Gates of Gaza (16:3)

The Philistine leaders learned of Samson's presence in the city and plotted to kill him when the city gate was opened in the morning. But Samson arose at midnight and used his great strength to remove the door of the gate and carry it to the top of a nearby hill. The citizens would have seen the gate there and marveled at Samson's strength. It was another demonstration that Israel's God was keeping His covenant to them in holding the Philistines at bay. It may be that Samson had gone to Gaza actually looking for another "opportunity" to upset the Philistines (cf. 14:4).

Samson and Delilah (16:4-22)

The Gaza incident had caused the Philistines to target Samson more than ever. He had resumed his position as judge, probably in Zorah where he had grown up. And once again Samson fell prey to his lust. The woman's name was Delilah and she lived in the nearby Valley of Sorek. Samson's relationships with Philistine women created occasions for God to inflict judgment on the Philistines, but at the same time they constituted moral sin for Samson in the sight of God. What happened this time has become one of the world's best-known stories of love betrayed.

The Philistines knew that Samson's extraordinary strength was supernatural and believed that there must be some secret to it. If they could find out what the secret was, perhaps they could use it to capture Samson. So the five lords of the Philistines approached Delilah and offered her a huge sum of money if she could entice Samson to reveal his secret. She did this in four acts based on lies and deceit. In each act Samson received nothing but momentary sexual gratification, and she received payment in silver. Each was using the relationship to exploit the other to satisfy his or her own desires.

The Philistines' Scheme (16:5)

The five lords of the Philistines each offered to give Delilah 1,100 pieces of silver that would make her a wealthy woman for life. Just ten pieces of silver would feed a person for a year (17:10). Her part was to entice Samson to reveal the secret of his strength and how it could be lost so that they might capture him and torture him. She soon put aside any romantic interest she had in Samson, lured by the chance to be wealthy.

The Game of Enticement (16:6-17)

Delilah used words of love and feminine charm to disarm Samson's defenses and then to discover his secret as if she were playing a game. For his part, Samson had nothing to gain but sexual pleasure followed by blindness, slavery, and humiliation. He was more than willing to be charmed by her enticements as she patiently pulled him into her trap.

In the first stage of the game she asked an apparently innocent question about how his "great strength" could be curbed so that he could be bound with ropes. He playfully told her that if she bound him with seven fresh bowstrings, he would become weak. She obtained the bowstrings and stationed men to capture him. But when she cried out, "The Philistines are upon you, Samson!" he snapped the bowstrings easily (vv. 6-9). Delilah pretended to be hurt that he had mocked her. But when she was again in his arms she began with the second stage by pleading with him to reveal his secret. This time he told her that brand new ropes would do it. Delilah teased him into letting her bind him and then announced, "The Philistines are upon you, Samson!" When they came he proudly showed off his strength to her again and became further caught in her trap (vv. 10-12).

The Lord had departed from him, because he had departed from the Lord.

In the third stage, Samson thought he was still in control when he told her that he could be captured if his hair was woven into the web of her loom and was fastened with a pin. Notice that he was getting closer to the truth. Again she patiently arranged for the Philistines to come and announced to Samson that they were coming. Samson arrogantly broke away for the third time (vv. 13-14).

The End of the Game (16:18-20)

In the final stage, Delilah turned on all her charm. She complained that he had mocked her three times. She whispered over and over that if he really loved her he would tell her his secret. Finally he yielded, and told her that he was a Nazirite to God. One mark of his dedication to the Lord was his uncut hair. Then he told her something not yet revealed in the biblical record—that if his head was shaved, his strength would leave him. Delilah knew that this time he had told her the truth. She informed the Philistines to come and bring the silver payment. She lulled Samson to sleep in her lap and engaged a barber to shave his head. Then she woke him calling out, "The Philistines are upon you, Samson!" He thought he would master them as he had before, but what he did not know was that the Spirit of the Lord had left him.

Think of Samson's moral sin, his foolish confidence in his strength, his going to sleep with his head in the lap of his enemy. Most tragic, he presumed God would honor his foolishness. The Lord had departed from *him*, not because he had a haircut, but because *he* had departed from the Lord. That is the tragedy of the whole story. Samson's game with Delilah was over and he had lost. Worse still he had lost touch with God, lost the presence of God in his life, and lost his freedom.

Samson's Imprisonment (16:21)

That night the Philistines made him a prisoner and led him forty miles south to Gaza. They gouged out his eyes—the physical means through which he had so often succumbed to sin—and harnessed him like an animal. Then they made him haul a grindstone while the passers-by mocked and jeered. From being a judge in Israel he sank to doing the work of a donkey. None of us should miss the truth that we too can easily fall into moral failure and disobedience to God. Stepping out of fellowship with God can permanently ruin our testimony. Samson's blindness because of sin remained, illustrating for us that though sins can be forgiven, the effects of them—the scars—may remain.

Though sins can be forgiven, the effects of them—the scars—may remain.

Hope for the Prisoner (16:22)

One of the key words in the Samson story now reappears as a sign of hope. It's the Hebrew word *wayyahel* meaning "began." The word marks four turning points in Samson's life (13:5, 25; 16:19, 22).

Samson and the Temple of Dagon (16:23-31)

Samson realized the foolishness of his sin and returned to active faith in God. Meanwhile the lords of the Philistines arranged a feast at the temple of Dagon to celebrate Samson's capture. The temple was filled, and thousands more lined the roof. When excitement began to build, a little boy led Samson before the jeering crowd. Then they made Samson entertain them like a clown.

Samson asked to be taken to the two great supporting pillars of the temple arena (v. 26). Then Samson prayed to God: "Strengthen me only this once, O God." He prays as a forgiven man, dependent on God alone. God heard his prayer above the cacophony of the drunken crowd shouting insults at him.

Bracing himself between the pillars he pushed with all his might. The pillars cracked and the roof of the temple with all those on it fell down on those in the arena. The lords of the Philistines and all the people around them were crushed along with Samson, while those on the roof fell to their deaths. In this one event more people died than all the other exploits of Samson during his life. The Philistines had boasted, "Our god has given our enemy into our hand" (16:24). But their boasting ended when Samson's God enabled him to destroy them all.

LESSON 11 EXAM

Use the answer sheet that has been provided to complete your exam.

1. **Because of their idolatry, the Israelites had been oppressed by the Philistines for __________ years.**
   A. 20
   B. 30
   C. 40
   D. 50

2. **Samson demonstrated that**
   A. human strength can overcome the enemy.
   B. dependence on God is not necessary.
   C. God blesses our acts of revenge.
   D. one man enabled by God could make a difference.

3. **In revenge for the murder of his wife, Samson**
   A. attacked the Philistines with a great slaughter.
   B. tied the tails of foxes together and burned the fields.
   C. gathered an army of Israelites and attacked Timnah.
   D. forced the Philistines to return the wedding garments.

4. **Three thousand men of Judah came to arrest Samson because they**
   A. were afraid of him.
   B. wanted to take him into protective custody.
   C. were intimidated by the Philistines.
   D. were resentful of his great strength.

5. **God answered Samson's prayer for water by**
   A. sending a friend with a flask of water.
   B. opening a seam in the rock in Lehi.
   C. showing him a spring nearby.
   D. transporting him to a flowing river.

6. **During the 20 years that Samson judged Israel**
   A. the land had rest.
   B. the Philistines were confined to their own territory.
   C. the Israelites returned whole-heartedly to the Lord.
   D. the Philistines were still in the land.

7. **Samson escaped from the Philistine city of Gaza by**
   A. calling the Israelites to come and rescue him.
   B. digging a hole under the wall and slipping by the guard.
   C. removing the door of the gate and carrying it to the top of the hill.
   D. disguising himself and walking calmly through the crowd.

8. **The relationship between Samson and Delilah was based on**
   A. exploitation.
   B. love.
   C. envy.
   D. politics.

9. **When the Spirit of God departed from Samson**
   A. he immediately sensed it.
   B. he did not discern it.
   C. he did not care.
   D. he realized he had no strength.

10. **When Samson prayed to God for strength to take revenge for the loss of his sight,**
    A. God could not hear him above the noise in the temple.
    B. God heard him and granted his request.
    C. God refused Samson his request.
    D. God only gave him strength to kill himself, not avenge himself.

What Do You Say?

From the life of Samson, what warnings/lessons would you pass on to young people?

LESSON 12

Spiritual and Moral Failure

Judges 17:1–21:25

The book of Judges records the downward cycles of Israel's national life after Joshua died. Each cycle begins with their spiritual and moral failure in forsaking the Lord and doing evil in His sight (cf. 3:7; 10:6 etc.). The failure in each cycle was worse than the one before. The final five chapters are an appendix and supply two stories from those times. The first illustrates their *spiritual failure* when they "abandoned the LORD" (2:12-13; 10:6). The second illustrates their *moral failure* when they did evil in the sight of the Lord (3:7, 13:1). It appears that the events in these stories took place early in the period of the judges, and they illustrate for the reader what happens when we forsake God and live in disobedience to His Word.

Everyone Did What Was Right in His Own Eyes

The key to these stories is a double phrase that occurs twice in each of them: "In those days there was no king in Israel. Everyone did what was right in his own eyes" (17:6; 18:1; 19:1 and 21:25). The statement that there was "no king" implies that the Israelites had rejected the Lord as their king by rejecting His law (1 Sam. 8:7). Having rejected God's law and authority, they practiced idolatry and immorality that seemed right in their own eyes. The phrase also means that they had no human government authority to hold back their downward slide. From being God's holy nation, Israel became an unholy and dysfunctional nation. By the time Samuel's sons became judges, even they turned "aside after gain. They took bribes

The failure in each cycle was worse than the one before.

and perverted justice" (1 Sam. 8:1-3). The national elders then concluded that the solution was to have a human king (1 Sam. 8:5). But when Saul became their king it wasn't long before the kings themselves led the nation into idolatry and immorality rather than resisting it.

The phrase "Everyone did what was right in his own eyes" is borrowed from the language of Moses (Deut. 12:8). Moses saw it in contrast to "doing what is right in the sight of the LORD" (Deut 12:25). When God's authority is rejected, and humans becomes the sole judges of what is right, there will be both spiritual and moral confusion and ultimately the collapse of ordered society. It is this sad truth that is illustrated by the two stories in chapters 17 to 21.

The Apostasy of Micah (17:1-6)

The story of Micah in chapters 17 and 18 is an example of their spiritual failure. Micah lived in Ephraim with his mother and stole 1,100 pieces of silver from her. When he heard her pronounce a curse on the thief, he confessed his crime and returned the silver. She then pronounced a blessing from God on him and declared that she had dedicated all her silver "to the LORD." With part of the silver she paid a silversmith to make two silver idols—one carved and the other cast (Ex. 20:4-5). Micah placed them in a shrine, literally, a "house of god." His shrine with its idol gods should be seen as false, compared to the true "house of God," that is, the tabernacle in Shiloh, only a few miles away (18:31).

Micah also made a priestly garment called an ephod, and some household idols. Then he consecrated one of his own sons as a priest. The incident is filled with moral and spiritual confusion of stealing, lying, idolatry, and false religion. It ends with, "Everyone did what was right in his own eyes" (v. 6).

Micah Establishes a False Priesthood (17:7-13)

The story then introduces us to a man named Jonathan (named in 18:30). He was a Levite, set aside for service in the tabernacle. But Jonathan was discontented with his God-ordained calling as a Levite and his home in Bethlehem, so he went to look for something better. In his travels through the hills of Ephraim, he found lodging overnight in Micah's house. He told Micah that he was looking for a better job. Micah then offered him a salary and benefits if he would stay with him and become his priest to care for the idols and to dispense counsel. Jonathan accepted the job and became like a son to Micah. Then Micah declared, "Now I know that the LORD will prosper me, because I have a Levite as priest" (vv. 7-13). But God had commanded the Levites to serve the priesthood of Aaron, but never to offer sacrifices and offerings (cf. Num. 3:1-39). It appears that Micah was reasoning that his pagan shrine with its pagan idols and false priest might bring him some special favor with God. He ignored the spiritual realities connected with the true tabernacle in nearby Shiloh.

Micah wanted to have gods that he could control and a self-made religion to meet his needs. The very essence of idolatry is creating and controlling gods for man's benefit (v. 13). In the contemporary world, people are looking for gods that serve them. Their gods today may be material things such as homes and cars and clothes. Idols may also be non-material things such as success in business, knowledge, or any field of endeavor. We can even make gods of family members, Bible knowledge, Christian service, or our jobs in the workplace. When anything other than God and the Lord Jesus Christ takes first place in our affections, it is idolatry. The apostle Paul defined covetousness as idolatry in Colossians 3:5, and the apostle John warned his readers, "Little children, keep yourselves from idols" (1 John 5:21). Micah's idolatry was also apostasy—turning away from God. It was the neglect of God's covenant, and the practice of that which was right in his own eyes (v. 6). His new religion was conjured up in his mind, paid for with his money, and its purpose was to benefit him alone (vv. 7-13). And he deceived himself into thinking that the true God would "prosper" him!

When anything other than God and the Lord Jesus Christ takes first place in our affections, it is idolatry.

The Danites Search for a Better Land (18:1-7)

Chapter 17 described the false religion of Micah. Chapter 18 builds on Micah's apostasy to show its effect on the spiritual decline and failure of the tribe of Dan, leading to its disappearance from the narrative of redemption history. The people of the tribe of Dan had failed to possess their inheritance from the Amorites and the Philistines who lived there. They were unwilling to trust the Lord to drive them out. So they retreated into the hill country of Judah (1:34-35). They were unhappy there, so they looked for a new homeland. They chose five warrior/spies from the area where Samson would later live. Their job was to look for a better land in the north.

On their way through the territory of Ephraim they lodged in Micah's house and met his Levite priest (vv. 1-4). The five Danites asked him to enquire of God to find out if they would prosper on their quest (v. 5). The Levite, no doubt wearing the ephod and claiming to speak for God, told them to "go in peace" (v. 6). Notice, however, that they had not gone to the tabernacle in Shiloh, where the Lord had established His Name (Deut. 16:2, 6, 11). The five spies continued on to the city of Laish in the far north at the foot of Mount Hermon. It did not have walls and appeared easy to invade.

The Report of the Five Spies (18:8-10)

The five spies went to Dan and recommended that they immediately take Laish by force and make it their home. They argued that they should "possess the land" because "God had given it" to them, probably based on Micah's prophecy. Their goal was to settle down in ease and prosperity, but they were not willing to trust God for the inheritance that He had chosen. They wanted what God had not given them and in the end they lost even their identity as the tribe of Dan. (cf. Rev. 7:5-8). Like many professing Christians today, they failed to possess what God had given them as an inheritance and were trying to acquire what God had not given them.

The Abduction of Micah's Idols and His Priest (18:11-26)

Six hundred warriors from Dan started northward from their hometowns of Zorah and Eshtaol. On the way they came to the home of Micah in Ephraim (v. 13). The five spies reminded them that Micah had a priest, an ephod, idols, and images and asked them to consider what to do (v. 14). They should have immediately executed Micah and the Levite (Deut. 13:6-11), but instead they took Micah's images. When the Levite priest questioned them, they asked him to become *their* priest. The Levite gladly accepted their offer and brought with him the ephod, idols, and images (vv. 19-20). The theft of the idols is emphasized by mentioning it five times (vv. 17-18, 23-24 and 27). Micah tried to recover what had been stolen without success. There isn't a single character in the story with any integrity.

The Danites Settle in Laish (18:27-31)

The Danites attacked the unguarded city of Laish and burned it. Then they rebuilt the city and called it "Dan" after their tribal patriarch.

They set up the carved image as an idol, and we learn that the name of the Levite false priest was Jonathan, a descendant of Moses (Ex. 2:21-22). Thus the climax of this story of apostasy is that the main perpetrator of it is a descendant of none other than Moses, Israel's great and godly leader.

Verse 30 contrasts the apostate worship at the site of Dan in the north with the true worship of the Lord and the true priesthood at the tabernacle in Shiloh.

The Moral Failure of Israel (Judges 19–21)

The final three chapters in Judges form a separate story and they illustrate the moral failure in the period of the judges. The refrain, "There was no king in Israel," appears two more times at the beginning and ending of this section (19:1; 21:25). The significance of it is that there was no authority in the land that would stem the flood of moral anarchy. It brings to a climax the idea that every person did what was right in his own eyes (21:25).

It is significant that in both of the final stories in the book of Judges, a Levite is prominent. They were men supposedly dedicated to the service of God in the tabernacle. But they both had exchanged that holy service for spiritual and moral depravity. In the first story it was a Levite from Bethlehem in Judah who usurped the office of a priest. Now in the second it was a Levite living in Ephraim who handed over his concubine to be gang-raped in order to save his own life.

A Levite and His Concubine (19:1-21)

An unnamed Levite was living in the hill country of Ephraim with his concubine—a legal, but secondary wife. She was unfaithful to him, and consequently returned to her father's home in Bethlehem. The Levite followed her there, trying to win her back. Her father encouraged reconciliation between his daughter and the Levite. On the fifth day the Levite started homeward with his concubine and his servant. They stopped for the night in Gibeah in the tribal area of Benjamin. At the town square they would expect a local family to show them hospitality. Instead, the townsfolk ignored them until an old man from the tribe of Ephraim insisted they stay with him (9:1-21). The Levite told him he was traveling north to offer a sacrifice in the tabernacle, presumably to make a thank offering for the return of his concubine.

The Atrocity Committed by the Benjamites in Gibeah (19:22-30)

The host and his guests were together when suddenly the house was surrounded by wicked men who demanded that the visitor be handed over to them for sexual immorality (cf. Gen. 19:5-8). The host pleaded with them not to act so wickedly and offered to hand over his own daughter and the Levite's concubine to them instead. The Levite then pushed his concubine out the door, where she was sexually abused all night long. He sacrificed her to save his own skin.

In the morning the Levite found her on the doorstep and ordered her to get up. When he realized she was dead, he took her body to his home in Ephraim. In a fit of vengeance he cut up her body into twelve pieces and summoned all Israel to respond to how she had been treated. Those who saw it concluded that nothing so horrible had ever been done in Israel since they had left Egypt.

Civil War Looming in Israel (20:1-17)

When the twelve tribes heard the story of Gibeah's crime and saw the evidence, they wanted revenge. Almost overnight, 400,000 men from every tribe except Benjamin assembled at Mizpah, a small town in Benjamin just five miles north of Gibeah. The Benjamites boycotted the meeting. The Israelites decided that ...

- no one would return home until they destroyed Gibeah (v. 8).
- instead of obeying God's law in the matter, they would deal with Benjamin by casting lots (Deut. 13:12-18).
- no Israelite would allow his daughter to marry a Benjamite (cf. 21:1).

They then asked the Benjamites to hand over the perpetrators of the atrocity. The Benjamites refused and prepared for civil war. Their attitude shows how deeply the culture of Canaan had infected them. They gathered an army of 26,000 warriors in Gibeah to resist the 400,000 from the other eleven tribes based in Mizpah.

The Battles against Benjamin (20:18-48)

The army of Israel made three attacks against Benjamin that followed the same pattern. Each begins with a request for counsel from God via the high priest (cf. v. 28). God specifically answered each of Israel's requests leading to their attack on Benjamin.

Before the first battle they enquired, "Who shall go up first for us?" God answered, "Judah shall go up first." This was appropriate because the victims of the atrocity were from Bethlehem in Judah. When the first day's battle was over, Judah had lost 22,000 men (vv. 18-21). When the battle was lost the eleven tribes came weeping before the Lord until evening. As the second battle loomed, Israel again asked for a word from God through the high priest saying, "Shall we again draw near to fight against our brothers, the people of Benjamin?" The Lord answered, "Go up against them." But when they did, the army of Israel lost another 18,000 warriors (vv. 22-25). The Lord was evidently teaching them through their losses not to depend on their own strength, but on His. It should be noted that God had confirmed to Israel they should go up against Benjamin but had not promised victory.

Before the third battle, eleven tribes came to the tabernacle once again and wept before God (vv. 26-48). They were desperate by this time because victory had eluded them. They fasted all that day long and offered burnt offerings and peace offerings to Him. This time Phinehas (as the high priest who stood before the ark) prayed, "Shall we go out once more to battle against our brothers, the people of Benjamin, or shall we cease?" This time the Lord's answer was, "Go up, for tomorrow I will give them into your hand." probably because of their humble attitude. When the battle was joined, the Benjamites came out of the city to fight, not knowing that an ambush had been set. The Israelites fell back as before to draw them out. But when the signal came, the main army turned around and attacked.

One sin had led to far-reaching consequences.

That day the Lord allowed the Israelites to defeat the Benjamites and 25,100 of them were killed. After that the Israelites went through all the towns in Benjamin and "struck them with the edge of the sword" and "all the towns that they found they set on fire." Only six hundred Benjamites escaped—by hiding in a hill east of Bethel with many caves called the Rock of Rimmon. The three battles had cost a total of 65,100 lives, the result of one moral atrocity and the stubborn pride of the Benjamites. One sin had led to far-reaching consequences.

The Survival of Benjamin in Jeopardy (21:1-4)

The Israelites then realized that the men of Benjamin were all dead except for the six hundred in hiding, and there were no women left alive. They had vowed that no Israelite woman could marry a Benjamite, which meant that the tribe of Benjamin would disappear. Instead of celebrating, they went to Shiloh once more to weep before the Lord. They cried out to Him, asking why all this had come upon them. They grieved that "there should be one tribe lacking in Israel" Although it was their own fault, at least they did turn to God in the crisis. They built an altar and offered burnt offerings Him.

Israel's First "Solution" to Benjamin's Jeopardy (21:5-14)

Then the Israelites remembered that when they made the call to arms, anyone who did not respond would be guilty of the death penalty. Now considering Benjamin's dilemma, they decided on a way to obtain wives for the six hundred men without seeking the Lord's will. They found that the men from the city of Jabesh Gilead, east of the Jordan, had not come (vv. 5-9; cf. 20:1). They decided to send warriors to destroy everyone in Jabesh Gilead except for the virgins of marriageable age whom they brought to Shiloh (cf. Num. 31:17-18). In the massacre that followed they saved four hundred of these girls (vv. 10-12). Then they offered peace to the Benjamites hiding at the Rock Rimmon, and wives to take back to their homes in Benjamin. There they could resume normal life again. But two hundred were still without wives.

Everything they did was technically correct, but morally corrupt.

Israel's Second "Solution" to Benjamin's Jeopardy (21:15-23)

The Israelites discovered a "technical loophole" by which the two hundred Benjamites could legitimately obtain wives. If they kidnapped Israelite virgins, it would absolve their parents from the curse for giving their daughters Benjamites. So they arranged for the two hundred Benjamite men to hide in the vineyards near Shiloh during a Jewish festival. Then when the virgins were singing and dancing before the Lord, the men came out of hiding and each abducted a wife for himself. When their relatives complained, the Israelites explained that their action was necessary because there was no other way to save the tribe of Benjamin.

Doing What Was Right in Their Own Eyes (21:24-25)

Thus their foolish oath and their stubbornness to stick to it had caused wicked mayhem in Israel. They used the name of God and pretended to be religious, but were acting like the Canaanites with no moral conscience. Everything they did was technically correct, but morally corrupt. They did what was right in their own eyes, their own view. In spite of their increasing godlessness, the tribe of Benjamin was indeed rescued. Two notable biblical characters who descended from the tribe of Benjamin were Saul, the first king in Israel (1 Sam. 9:1-2), and Paul, the Apostle to the Gentiles (Rom. 11:1).

The Immorality of Israel and the Benjamites

Consider again the extreme moral degradation of these final chapters. The gang rape and murder of an innocent woman, the dismemberment of the victim's body, the proud defense of guilty men, the ensuing war against Benjamin, the capture of four hundred innocent virgins and the kidnapping of two hundred more. The whole series of incidents is an example of the moral collapse of the entire nation of Israel.

These last five chapters bring the book of Judges to a climax of spiritual and moral catastrophe. They graphically illustrate in practically every detail that God's people were doing what was right in their own eyes. It is no accident that these last five chapters both begin and end with this phrase (17:6; 21:25). The reason for the immoral outcome was their spiritual failure in that they "forsook the Lord" (2:12), and their moral failure in that they "did evil in the sight of the Lord" (13:1).

LESSON 12 EXAM

Use the answer sheet that has been provided to complete your exam.

1. **The last five chapters of the book of Judges are**
   A. accounts of events that took place after Samson died.
   B. accounts of events that took place early in the times of the judges.
   C. so bizarre that they can't have really happened.
   D. the author's attempt to illustrate the purpose of his book.

2. **These final chapters illustrate**
   A. God's rejection of people when they forsake Him.
   B. the moral integrity of the Israelites.
   C. what happens when we forsake God and live in disobedience to Him.
   D. the gradual growth in the Israelites understanding of God.

3. **The story of Micah is an example of the Israelites'**
   A. spiritual failure.
   B. moral failure.
   C. spiritual growth.
   D. concern for the Canaanites.

4. **Micah __________ to earn God's favor.**
   A. worshipped at the tabernacle
   B. hired a priest
   C. took care of his mother
   D. paid his tithe

5. **Idolatry is defined as**
   A. bowing down to a god in a pagan temple.
   B. guiding your life by worldly principles.
   C. refusing to believe that God exists.
   D. having something other than God that takes first place in our affections.

6. **The final three chapters of Judges are about**
   A. repentance and restoration .
   B. moral failure.
   C. God's rejection of His people.
   D. the establishment of a kingdom.

7. **Civil war broke out in Israel when**
   A. two tribes wanted to become a separate country.
   B. the Benjamites refused to hand over the men of Gibeah for punishment.
   C. Judah moved the tabernacle to their territory.
   D. the Levites rebelled against the high priest.

8. **In the final battle, only __________ Benjamites escaped.**
   A. 30
   B. 200
   C. 400
   D. 600

9. **The tribe of Benjamin was saved from extinction by**
   A. murder and kidnapping.
   B. changing the law.
   C. marriage with Canaanite women.
   D. God's direct intervention.

10. **Two prominent descendants of the tribe of Benjamin were**
    A. King David and Barnabas.
    B. Isaiah and the apostle Peter.
    C. King Saul and the apostle Paul.
    D. Jeremiah and Timothy.

What Do You Say?

How does the phrase, "In those days there was no king in Israel; everyone did what was right in his own eyes," explain Israel's decline? What are the ramifications of this concept for society today?

The Lord is not slow to fulfill His promise as some count slowness, but is patient toward you, not wishing that any should perish, but that all should reach repentance.

—2 Peter 3:9

Made in the USA
Coppell, TX
19 January 2026